YOUR C
AQUARIUS 2024
PERSONAL
HOROSCOPE

Monthly Astrological Prediction Forecast Readings of
Every Zodiac Astrology Sun Star Signs- Love,
Romance, Money, Finances, Career, Health, Travel,
Spirituality.

Iris Quinn

Alpha Zuriel Publishing

Your Complete Aquarius 2024 Personal Horoscope/ Iris Quinn. -- 1st ed.

"In the dance of the planets, we find the rhythms of life. Astrology reminds us that we are all connected to the greater universe, and our actions have ripple effects throughout the cosmos."
— IRIS QUINN

CONTENTS

CHAPTER ONE

AQUARIUS PROFILE

- Constellation: Aquarius
- Zodiac symbol: Water Bearer
- Date: January 20 – February 18
- Element: Air
- Ruling Planet: Uranus (Traditional), Saturn (Modern)
- Career Planet: Uranus
- Love Planet: Venus
- Money Planet: Jupiter
- Planet of Fun, Entertainment, Creativity, and Speculations: Uranus
- Planet of Health and Work: Saturn
- Planet of Home and Family Life: Moon
- Planet of Spirituality: Neptune
- Planet of Travel, Education, Religion, and Philosophy: Jupiter

Colors:
- Colors: Electric Blue, Turquoise

- Colors that promote love, romance, and social harmony: Pastel Shades
- Color that promotes earning power: Silver

Gem: Amethyst
Metals: Aluminum
Scent: Orchid
Birthstone: Amethyst

Qualities:
• Quality: Fixed (represents stability)
• Quality most needed for balance: Flexibility

Strongest Virtues:
• Intellectual curiosity
• Open-mindedness
• Originality
• Independence
• Altruism

Deepest Need: Freedom

Characteristics to Avoid:
• Stubbornness
• Rebellion for the sake of rebellion
• Detachment
• Emotional aloofness

Signs of Greatest Overall Compatibility:
• Gemini
• Libra

Signs of Greatest Overall Incompatibility:
• Taurus
• Scorpio
• Cancer

- Sign Most Supportive for Career Advancement: Aries
- Sign Most Supportive for Emotional Well-being: Libra
- Sign Most Supportive Financially: Taurus
- Sign Best for Marriage and/or Partnerships: Leo
- Sign Most Supportive for Creative Projects: Gemini
- Best Sign to Have Fun With: Sagittarius

Signs Most Supportive in Spiritual Matters:
• Pisces
• Cancer

Best Day of the Week: Saturday

AQUARIUS TRAITS

- Intellectual and innovative thinker
- Independent and free-spirited nature
- Friendly and sociable personality
- Emotionally detached at times
- Stubborn and resistant to change.
- Humanitarian and altruistic mindset
- Tendency to be unpredictable or eccentric in behavior.

PERSONALITY OF AQUARIUS

Aquarius individuals possess a captivating and enigmatic personality that sets them apart from the crowd. They are known for their unique perspective and unconventional approach to life. Here are some aspects of the Aquarius personality that flow seamlessly together:

With their independent spirit, Aquarius individuals march to the beat of their own drum. They value their freedom and resist conforming to societal norms. Their intellectual prowess shines through as they eagerly explore new ideas and concepts, delving into the realms of science, technology, and philosophy.

Deeply driven by a sense of compassion, Aquarius individuals are natural humanitarians. They possess a genuine desire to make a positive impact on the world around them. Their hearts are drawn to social causes, and they actively participate in activism and volunteer work, always striving to create a better and more equitable society.

Open-mindedness is a defining trait of Aquarius individuals. They embrace diversity and appreciate the beauty of different perspectives. Their minds are receptive to unconventional ideas, and they are unafraid to challenge the status quo, fueling their quest for a more progressive world.

Though their rationality often takes precedence, Aquarius individuals have a hidden depth of emotions. They may appear detached at times, but beneath the surface lies a rich inner world. They navigate their feelings intellectually, using their logical approach to understand and process their emotions.

Aquarius individuals are social butterflies, effortlessly engaging with others and expanding their network. Their friendly nature and intellectual prowess draw people to them, as they relish in thought-provoking conversations and the exchange of ideas. Their wide circle of friends spans across different backgrounds and interests, reflecting their appreciation for diversity.

In relationships, Aquarius individuals seek partners who respect their need for independence and intellectual stimulation. They value a strong mental connection and appreciate a partner who shares their vision for a better world. While they may struggle with emotional vulnerability, they are fiercely loyal and committed to nurturing a deep and meaningful partnership.

WEAKNESSES OF AQUARIUS

The Aquarius personality, like any other, has its share of weaknesses that emerge within the depths of their complex character. As they navigate through life's challenges, some tendencies may manifest, potentially hindering their growth and relationships. Let us explore these aspects as they flow naturally:

At times, Aquarius individuals may become emotionally detached, struggling to fully connect with their own emotions and those of others. Their rationality and intellectual approach to life can overshadow their ability to empathize on a deep emotional level. This detachment may lead to difficulties in forming intimate bonds and understanding the emotional needs of their loved ones.

In their pursuit of freedom and independence, Aquarius individuals may exhibit a rebellious streak. Their resistance to authority and established structures can sometimes lead them to question rules and boundaries, even when they are in place for their own well-being. This rebellion can create friction in certain situations, potentially causing strain in relationships and professional environments.

Aquarius individuals, driven by their strong convictions and ideals, may become uncompromising in their beliefs. They may struggle to see alternative perspectives and can be resistant to changing their viewpoints. This rigidity may hinder their ability to adapt to new circumstances and engage in constructive dialogue with others.

While Aquarius individuals are often visionary thinkers, their ideas can sometimes be perceived as too unconventional or impractical by others. Their forward-thinking nature may cause them to overlook the practical aspects of implementing their ideas, leading to difficulties in turning their visions into tangible realities.

Due to their independent nature, Aquarius individuals may resist asking for help or support when they need it. They may perceive seeking assistance as a sign of weakness or dependence, leading them to shoulder burdens alone. This self-reliance can sometimes result in feelings of isolation and overwhelm.

It is important to remember that these weaknesses are not inherent flaws but rather aspects that Aquarius individuals can work on to achieve personal growth and stronger connections with others. Recognizing and addressing these tendencies can lead to a more balanced and fulfilling life for Aquarius individuals.

RELATIONSHIP COMPATIBILITY WITH AQUARIUS

Based only on their Sun signs, this is how Aquarius interacts with others. These are the compatibility interpretations for all 12 potential Aquarius combinations. This is a limited and insufficient method of determining compatibility.

However, Sun-sign compatibility remains the foundation for overall harmony in a relationship.

The general rule is that yin and yang do not get along. Yin complements yin, and yang complements yang. While yin and yang partnerships can be successful, they require more effort. Earth and water zodiac signs are both Yin. Yang is represented by the fire and air zodiac signs.

Aquarius (Yang) and Aries (Yang):

When an Aquarius individual comes together with an Aries partner, their shared Yang energy creates a dynamic and exciting relationship. Both signs are independent, forward-thinking, and adventurous,

11

which can lead to a vibrant and stimulating connection. They appreciate each other's individuality and support each other's aspirations and goals. However, clashes may arise due to their strong personalities and occasional stubbornness. Both Aquarius and Aries need to find a balance between their independence and the need for compromise to ensure a harmonious partnership. With open communication and a willingness to understand each other's perspectives, they can build a relationship filled with shared adventures and personal growth.

Aquarius (Yang) and Taurus (Yin):

When Aquarius and Taurus come together, their contrasting energies create a unique blend of stability and innovation. Aquarius, with their progressive and intellectual nature, brings fresh ideas and a sense of adventure to the relationship, while Taurus provides grounding and a practical approach. They can learn from each other and find a balance between spontaneity and security. However, conflicts may arise due to Taurus' desire for routine and stability conflicting with Aquarius' need for change and excitement. Both partners must embrace compromise and flexibility to create a lasting and fulfilling partnership. By appreciating each other's strengths and fostering open communication, they can cultivate a relationship that combines stability and growth.

Aquarius (Yang) and Gemini (Yang):

When Aquarius and Gemini join forces, their shared Yang energy ignites a stimulating and intellectually charged relationship. They share a love for mental stimulation, communication, and exploring new ideas. They engage in deep conversations and enjoy each other's wit and intellect. Both signs are social and outgoing, which allows them to thrive in a vibrant social life together. However, challenges may arise when it comes to emotional depth and commitment. Both Aquarius and Gemini tend to prioritize freedom and independence, which can sometimes create distance in their relationship. By nurturing emotional intimacy and creating a safe space for vulnerability, they can build a strong bond that balances intellectual connection and emotional depth.

Aquarius (Yang) and Cancer (Yin):

Aquarius and Cancer bring together contrasting energies in their relationship. Aquarius, with its independent and intellectual nature, may find it challenging to understand Cancer's emotional depth and sensitivity. Cancer, on the other hand, seeks security and emotional connection, which can clash with Aquarius' need for freedom and space. Both partners must work on communication and empathy to bridge these differences. With patience, understanding, and a willingness to compromise, they can create a harmonious relationship that respects each other's needs for emotional security and personal freedom.

Aquarius (Yang) and Leo (Yang):

Aquarius and Leo share a dynamic and lively connection filled with passion and creativity. Both signs are confident, outgoing, and enjoy being in the spotlight. They inspire each other to pursue their dreams and support each other's individuality. However, clashes may occur due to their strong personalities and occasional power struggles. Aquarius' independent nature may challenge Leo's desire for attention and admiration, while Leo's need for constant validation may conflict with Aquarius' need for personal freedom. By learning to appreciate and celebrate each other's strengths, they can create a vibrant and mutually fulfilling partnership.

Aquarius (Yang) and Virgo (Yin):

Aquarius and Virgo bring together contrasting energies in their relationship. Aquarius is innovative, visionary, and values intellectual pursuits, while Virgo is practical, detail-oriented, and focused on organization. These differences can lead to both challenges and opportunities for growth. Aquarius may find Virgo's attention to detail and perfectionism to be stifling, while Virgo may struggle with Aquarius' occasional detachment and need for independence. Both partners need to communicate openly, appreciate each other's strengths, and find a balance between spontaneity and practicality. With patience and understanding, they can build a relationship that combines intellectual stimulation with grounded stability.

Aquarius (Yang) and Libra (Yang):

Aquarius and Libra share a natural affinity for intellectual pursuits, social connections, and a desire for harmony. They appreciate each other's ideas, enjoy engaging in stimulating conversations, and value the power of diplomacy in their relationship. However, conflicts may arise due to their indecisiveness and a tendency to avoid confrontations. Both partners need to work on making firm decisions and addressing issues head-on to maintain a healthy balance. By cultivating open communication, embracing compromise, and nurturing their intellectual connection, they can create a harmonious and intellectually fulfilling partnership.

Aquarius (Yang) and Scorpio (Yin):

Aquarius and Scorpio possess contrasting energies, which can create a dynamic and intense relationship. Aquarius is independent, open-minded, and values personal freedom, while Scorpio is passionate, emotional, and seeks deep connections. These differences can lead to both attraction and challenges. Aquarius may find Scorpio's intensity and possessiveness overwhelming, while Scorpio may struggle with Aquarius' need for space and detachment. Both partners must learn to navigate their differences and find a balance between emotional depth and personal freedom. With trust, communication, and mutual respect, they can create a powerful and transformative partnership.

Aquarius (Yang) and Sagittarius (Yang):

Aquarius and Sagittarius share a zest for life, a love for adventure, and a mutual understanding of each other's need for personal freedom. They enjoy exploring new horizons, engaging in intellectual discussions, and supporting each other's aspirations. Both signs value independence and possess an optimistic outlook on life. However, conflicts may arise when it comes to commitment and emotional depth. Both Aquarius and Sagittarius may struggle with the idea of settling down and may prioritize their individual pursuits over relationship responsibilities. By fostering open communication, embracing shared adventures, and respecting each other's need for independence, they can create a vibrant and fulfilling partnership.

Aquarius (Yang) and Capricorn (Yin):

Aquarius and Capricorn bring together contrasting energies in their relationship. Aquarius is innovative, forward-thinking, and values personal freedom, while Capricorn is practical, ambitious, and focused on traditional values. These differences can create both challenges and opportunities for growth. Aquarius may find Capricorn's serious and conventional nature to be restrictive, while Capricorn may struggle with Aquarius' need for constant change and unconventional ideas. Both partners need to find a balance between structure and spontaneity, embracing each other's unique perspectives, and working towards common goals. With patience, understanding, and mutual support, they can create a harmonious and balanced partnership.

Aquarius (Yang) and Aquarius (Yang):

When two Aquarius individuals come together, their shared Yang energy creates a relationship filled with intellectual stimulation, innovation, and a deep understanding of each other's need for personal freedom. They enjoy engaging in deep conversations, exploring new ideas, and supporting each other's individuality. However, conflicts may arise due to their strong personalities and occasional clashes of egos. Both partners need to practice open communication, compromise, and respect each other's need for independence. By embracing their shared values and nurturing their intellectual connection, they can build a progressive and fulfilling partnership.

Aquarius (Yang) and Pisces (Yin):

Aquarius and Pisces possess contrasting energies, which can create a complex and intriguing relationship. Aquarius is rational, intellectual, and values personal freedom, while Pisces is intuitive, emotional, and seeks spiritual connections. These differences can lead to both challenges and opportunities for growth. Aquarius may find Pisces' emotional depth and sensitivity overwhelming, while Pisces may struggle with Aquarius' occasional detachment and need for independence. Both partners need to navigate their differences with compassion, empathy, and open communication. By embracing their unique strengths and finding a balance between intellect and emotions, they can create a relationship that combines intellectual stimulation and profound emotional connection.

LOVE AND PASSION

In matters of love and passion, Aquarius individuals possess a distinct and captivating approach. Their unconventional nature and intellectual curiosity shape their experiences in relationships. Here are some aspects that contribute to their unique love and passion:

Aquarius individuals are drawn to the extraordinary. They seek partners who share their passion for intellectual exploration and who can engage them in deep and thought-provoking conversations. Mental stimulation is a key ingredient in their romantic connections.

Their love is rooted in a sense of friendship. Aquarius believes in building a strong foundation of friendship with their partner, valuing a deep connection and a sense of camaraderie. They appreciate a partner who can be both a lover and a confidant, someone they can share their hopes, dreams, and fears with.

Aquarius individuals value personal freedom and individuality. They require space and independence to nurture their own interests and passions. They seek partners who understand and support their need for autonomy, respecting their boundaries while allowing them room to explore their individuality.

Their love is often marked by an unconventional and open-minded approach. Aquarius individuals are willing to challenge societal norms and traditions in their relationships. They are attracted to partners who are open to exploring new ideas, alternative lifestyles, and unique experiences.

Aquarius individuals may have a tendency to be emotionally detached at times. While they possess a deep sense of empathy, they may struggle with expressing their emotions openly. It is important for their partners to provide a safe and understanding environment where Aquarius feels comfortable sharing their innermost feelings.

Their passion is ignited by the pursuit of knowledge and personal growth. Aquarius individuals thrive on continuous learning and expanding their horizons. They are attracted to partners who share their thirst for knowledge and who encourage their intellectual pursuits.

Overall, Aquarius individuals approach love and passion with a blend of intellectual curiosity, personal freedom, and a desire to challenge the status quo. They seek partners who embrace their unique perspective and are willing to embark on a journey of intellectual and emotional exploration together.

MARRIAGE

Aquarius individuals approach the institution of marriage with a generally supportive attitude. However, they prioritize ensuring their financial stability before fully committing to marriage. They understand the importance of a solid financial foundation to provide stability and security for themselves and their partners.

To maintain a healthy and fulfilling marriage, Aquarius individuals should be mindful of their tendency to engage in disputes and criticize their partners. It is crucial for them to temper these inclinations, as constant criticism can weaken their partner's morale and put the relationship at risk. Open and respectful communication is key to resolving conflicts and fostering a harmonious bond.

Aquarius individuals strive like no one else to keep their marriage alive. They are committed to the well-being and growth of their relationship, investing time and effort to nurture and strengthen their connection. However, if they find the disagreements to be insurmountable and compromising their happiness, they will not hesitate to consider ending the marriage.

In terms of responsibilities, Aquarius individuals value equality and fairness in their marital dynamics. They appreciate partners who share the load of both work and family duties. They seek order and efficiency in their marriage and approach their marital tasks with dedication and a positive attitude.

Aquarius males and females are dedicated and hardworking, valuing their roles as partners, parents, and spouses. They hold egalitarian values and strive for a balanced division of responsibilities, ensuring that their spouses do not carry an unfair burden. They reject sexism and work towards creating an environment of mutual support and respect within their marriage.

CHAPTER TWO

AQUARIUS 2024 HOROSCOPE

Overview Aquarius 2024

Aquarius, as you step into the year 2024, the cosmos is aligning in a way that will shape your journey in profound ways. The planetary movements throughout the year indicate a time of opportunities, challenges, and growth. The alignment of the Sun, Mercury, Venus, Mars, and Jupiter will play a crucial role in various aspects of your life, including your career, relationships, health, and personal development. Let's delve deeper into what the year has in store for you.

The year begins with a strong focus on your career. The conjunction between Mercury and Uranus in Taurus in May suggests a time of innovation and creativity in your professional life. You may find yourself taking on new projects or exploring new ideas that can lead to career growth. However, the square between Mars and Pluto in June indicates potential challenges and conflicts at work. It's important to stay focused and not let conflicts derail your progress.

As you move into the second quarter, the financial aspect takes center stage. The sextile between Venus and Chiron in June is a healing balm to any financial wounds you may have. This is a period of financial recuperation. Reassess your financial goals, and don't be afraid to make necessary adjustments. Networking is key during this period. The quintile between Venus and the True Node in June suggests that making the right connections can open doors to financial opportunities.

The third quarter of the year brings a mix of challenges and opportunities in your career. The conjunction between Mercury and Uranus in Taurus in May suggests a time of innovation and creativity in your professional life. You may find yourself taking on new projects or exploring new ideas that can lead to career growth. However, the square between Mars and Pluto in June indicates potential challenges and conflicts at work. It's important to stay focused and not let conflicts derail your progress.

As the year comes to a close, the focus shifts back to your financial life. The sextile between Venus and Chiron in June is a healing balm to any financial wounds you may have. This is a period of financial recuperation. Reassess your financial goals, and don't be afraid to make necessary adjustments. Networking is key during this period. The quintile between Venus and the True Node in June suggests that making the right connections can open doors to financial opportunities.

In terms of relationships and social life, the square between Venus and Neptune in June indicates a time of confusion or misunderstanding in your relationships. It's important to communicate clearly and honestly during this time and to seek clarity when needed. The sextile between Mercury and the True Node in June also suggests that communication and social interactions will be particularly important during this time. This is a good time to build and strengthen relationships.

As the year progresses, you will find that your social life picks up pace. There is a sense of camaraderie and belonging that envelops you. Engage in social activities, but be mindful of not overcommitting yourself. Balance is key.

Your health and wellness are areas that require attention this year. The sesquiquadrate between the Sun and Chiron in June is a call for healing. This is the time to integrate wellness practices into your daily routine. Whether it's through yoga, meditation, or simply spending time in nature, nurturing your well-being is essential.

The latter part of the year brings vitality. The sextile between the Sun and Chiron in June is a rejuvenating energy. Engage in physical activities that not only strengthen your body but also bring joy to your soul.

On a spiritual level, 2024 is a year of profound growth and learning. The quintile between Jupiter and Saturn in May is a cosmic classroom. This is a time of spiritual learning and seeking higher wisdom. You are being called to delve deeper into the mysteries of life.

The conjunction between Venus and Pluto in July is a catalyst for transformation. This is a period of shedding old skins and emerging anew. Embrace the changes and allow yourself to grow and evolve.

In conclusion, Aquarius, the year 2024 will be a year of growth, transformation, and self-discovery. While there will be challenges along the way, these challenges will provide opportunities for personal development and understanding. Embrace the journey

28

and make the most of the opportunities that come your way. Stay open to learning and growing, and don't be afraid to explore new paths. Your adventurous spirit will guide you through the ups and downs of the year, leading you to new heights in your personal and professional life.

Remember, the stars are merely guides. You have the power to shape your destiny. Use the insights from your horoscope to navigate the year, but always listen to your inner voice. It is your most reliable guide. Here's to a year filled with growth, success, and happiness.

January 2024

Horoscope

January is a month of transformative energy for Aquarius. The celestial alignments present a unique blend of opportunities and challenges that will shape various aspects of your life. As the month begins, you may experience a clash between your desires and responsibilities, indicated by Venus in Sagittarius squaring Saturn in Pisces on January 1st. This conflict could create a sense of frustration and hinder your ability to find balance.

However, on January 3rd, Venus forms a quincunx aspect with Jupiter, urging you to make adjustments in your love life. It's essential to be flexible and open-minded to navigate any relationship issues during this time. Simultaneously, Mercury quintiles Saturn, providing you with mental clarity and the ability to communicate effectively. Take advantage of this alignment to address any lingering misunderstandings or conflicts in your personal interactions.

Emotions may run high on January 9th as the Sun squares Chiron, bringing unresolved wounds to the surface. This can be a transformative period for healing and personal growth. Use this opportunity to reflect on past experiences and engage in self-care practices that promote emotional well-being.

The middle of the month holds promise for Aquarius in matters of love and relationships. On January 12th, Mars trines Jupiter, fueling your passion and confidence in romantic endeavors. This aspect brings harmonious energy, allowing you to express your desires with charisma and charm. It's an excellent time to deepen the connection with your partner or take bold steps toward finding a new love interest.

In summary, January presents a mix of challenges and opportunities for Aquarius. The key to navigating this month successfully lies in maintaining a flexible and open-minded approach. Prioritize self-care, exercise caution in financial matters, and embrace the transformative energy to foster personal growth and deeper connections in love and relationships.

Love

For Aquarius, love takes center stage in January as the celestial energies stimulate both challenges and opportunities in relationships. The month begins with Venus square Saturn, which may create tension and potential obstacles in your romantic life. You may feel restricted or weighed down by responsibilities, making it essential to find a balance between personal desires and commitments. Open and honest communication is crucial during this period to address any relationship issues and find mutually satisfying solutions.

On January 3rd, Venus forms a quincunx aspect with Jupiter, urging you to make adjustments in your approach to love and relationships. It's a time to be flexible and adaptable, as your expectations may need revision. Embracing compromise and seeking common ground will contribute to relationship harmony. Single Aquarians may find themselves drawn to individuals who challenge their usual preferences, leading to exciting and unexpected connections.

Mid-month brings a significant opportunity for love and romance. Mars trines Jupiter on January 12th, igniting passion and confidence in your interactions. Your charisma and magnetic personality will attract potential partners effortlessly. This alignment encourages you to take bold steps in matters of the heart. Whether you're starting a new relationship or deepening an existing one, this is a time of joy and fulfillment.

Towards the end of January, Venus squares Neptune, requiring caution in matters of love. Be mindful of idealizing partners or romanticizing situations without a solid foundation. Take the time to evaluate the authenticity and compatibility of a potential partner before fully committing. Trust your instincts and use discernment when navigating romantic opportunities.

Career

Aquarius individuals will experience a dynamic and transformative energy in their professional lives during January. The celestial aspects indicate a mix of challenges and opportunities that will shape your career trajectory.

At the beginning of the month, Venus squares Saturn, creating potential obstacles and limitations in your professional endeavors. You may face difficulties or delays in achieving your goals, leading to a sense of frustration or stagnation. However, perseverance and a strategic approach will help you overcome these challenges. Focus on the long-term vision and remain committed to your professional aspirations.

On January 3rd, Mercury quintiles Saturn, providing mental clarity and effective communication skills. This alignment favors negotiations, presentations, and collaborative projects. Utilize this period to express your ideas and make significant contributions to team efforts. Your insights and innovative thinking will be appreciated and recognized by colleagues and superiors.

The middle of January brings a surge of motivation and confidence in your career path. Mars trines Jupiter on January 12th, igniting your ambition and drive for success. This aspect encourages you to take calculated risks and assert yourself in professional situations. Seize opportunities for growth and advancement, as your determination and hard work will yield fruitful results.

Finance

Aquarius individuals will need to exercise caution and prudence in their financial matters during January. The celestial aspects indicate a need for careful planning and strategic decision-making to ensure stability and prosperity.

At the beginning of the month, Venus squares Saturn, highlighting potential financial limitations or obstacles. This aspect serves as a reminder to practice discipline and avoid impulsive spending. It's crucial to stick to a budget and prioritize essential expenses. Consider reviewing your financial goals and making necessary adjustments to align with your current circumstances.

On January 8th, Venus biquintiles Jupiter, offering a positive financial influence. This alignment can bring opportunities for growth and abundance. However, it's important to approach these opportunities with discernment and avoid excessive risk-taking. Make informed decisions and seek expert advice if needed to maximize your financial gains.

Mid-month brings a focus on long-term financial planning. Venus squares Neptune on January 19th, emphasizing the importance of clarity and practicality in your financial decisions. Be cautious of potential illusions or unrealistic expectations regarding investments or financial ventures. Take the time to thoroughly research and evaluate opportunities before committing your resources. It may also be beneficial to reassess your financial goals and ensure they align with your long-term aspirations.

Health

Maintaining optimal health and well-being should be a priority for Aquarius individuals in January. The celestial aspects highlight the importance of self-care and adopting healthy habits to support your physical and emotional well-being.

At the beginning of the month, Venus squares Saturn, which may contribute to a sense of low energy or fatigue. It's essential to listen to your body and ensure you're getting adequate rest and relaxation. Pay attention to any signs of stress or burnout and take necessary breaks to recharge. Incorporate stress-management techniques into your daily routine, such as meditation, yoga, or engaging in activities that bring you joy and relaxation.

On January 9th, the Sun squares Chiron, bringing attention to emotional well-being. This aspect may surface unresolved wounds or emotional challenges. It's important to acknowledge and address these issues to promote healing and personal growth. Consider seeking support from a therapist or counselor to navigate any emotional struggles effectively.

Mid-month brings a surge of vitality and physical energy. Mars trines Jupiter on January 12th, providing a boost of motivation and stamina. Take advantage of this energy by engaging in regular exercise and physical activities that you enjoy. This alignment also supports proactive approaches to maintaining overall health, such as adopting a nutritious diet and incorporating stress-reducing practices.

Towards the end of January, the Sun's semi-sextile with Saturn may contribute to a sense of fatigue or low energy. It's crucial to prioritize self-care during this period. Ensure you're getting sufficient sleep, nourishing your body with nutritious meals, and practicing mindfulness to support your overall well-being.

Remember to listen to your body's signals and honor your physical and emotional needs. Incorporate self-care practices that promote balance, relaxation, and rejuvenation. By prioritizing your health and well-being, you can navigate January with vitality and maintain a strong foundation for optimal health throughout the year.

Travel

For Aquarius individuals, January presents opportunities for travel and exploration. The celestial aspects indicate a sense of adventure and a desire for new experiences. However, it's important to plan your travels carefully and consider any potential challenges that may arise.

Mid-month, Mars trines Uranus, igniting a spirit of spontaneity and adventure. This alignment encourages you to embrace the unexpected and step out of your comfort zone. If you've been yearning for a change of scenery, this is an ideal time to plan a getaway or explore new destinations. Whether it's a weekend getaway or a more extended trip, allow yourself to indulge in new experiences and immerse yourself in different cultures.

While the desire for adventure is strong, it's crucial to balance it with practicality and preparation. Stay updated with travel advisories and be mindful of any potential disruptions or restrictions that may affect your plans. It's also advisable to have a flexible itinerary and backup plans in case of unforeseen circumstances.

Take the time to research and plan your travels carefully. Consider factors such as transportation, accommodations, and any cultural or safety considerations. Engage in responsible and sustainable travel practices, respecting the local customs and environment of the places you visit.

During your travels, embrace the opportunity to expand your horizons and learn from different cultures and perspectives. Be open to new experiences, connect with locals, and create memories that will enrich your personal growth.

If traveling is not feasible during this time, you can still explore new local attractions or engage in day trips to nearby destinations. Discover hidden gems in your own backyard and appreciate the beauty and diversity of your surroundings.

Insight from the stars

"Embrace the power of vulnerability and open your heart to deeper connections. It is through vulnerability that true intimacy is forged."

Best days of the month: `January 8th, 12th, 19th, 22nd, 25th, 28th and 30th.

February 2024

Horoscope

The month begins with Mars semi-square Saturn on February 2nd, presenting a challenge that tests your determination and resilience. This aspect encourages you to overcome obstacles and persevere towards your goals. The sextile between Mercury and Neptune on February 2nd enhances your intuition and communication skills, allowing you to express your ideas with clarity and compassion.

The latter half of February brings an emphasis on self-reflection and personal growth. The Mercury sextile Jupiter aspect on February 22nd amplifies your mental capabilities and expands your horizons. This alignment favors learning, teaching, and engaging in philosophical discussions. Embrace opportunities for intellectual growth and embrace the joy of lifelong learning.

Overall, February 2024 invites Aquarius individuals to embrace their uniqueness, seek personal growth, and expand their horizons. It's a month of self-discovery, enhanced communication, and the pursuit of innovative ideas. Embrace the transformative energy and trust in your ability to navigate the challenges and embrace the opportunities that lie ahead.

Love

The Sun's semi-sextile with Venus on February 5th infuses your relationships with warmth and affection. This aspect encourages romantic gestures, heartfelt conversations, and a deeper emotional connection with your partner. It's an excellent time to express your love and appreciation.

However, the Venus square Chiron aspect on the same day may bring up past wounds and emotional vulnerabilities within relationships. It's crucial to approach any conflicts or triggers with compassion, understanding, and a willingness to heal together. Use this opportunity to address any unresolved issues and foster a deeper sense of emotional intimacy.

On February 9th, Mercury's semi-sextile with Saturn urges you to communicate your needs and boundaries clearly. Open and honest conversations with your partner will help establish a solid foundation built on trust and respect. Remember to listen attentively to your partner's perspective and find mutually beneficial solutions.

As we move into the latter half of the month, the Sun's semi-square with True Node on February 20th may bring some challenges to relationships. It's essential to navigate these obstacles with patience and understanding. Avoid impulsive reactions and instead focus on finding a balanced compromise that honors both your individuality and your commitment to the relationship.

The Venus sextile True Node on February 29th enhances your social connections and brings opportunities for new romantic encounters or deepening existing bonds. You may find yourself drawn to individuals who share your vision for the future and who inspire you intellectually. Embrace these connections and allow love to unfold naturally.

Career

The conjunction between Venus and Mars on February 22nd ignites your ambition and drive, providing you with the energy and determination to pursue your career goals. This alignment empowers you to assert yourself confidently and take bold steps towards success.

The Mercury conjunction with Saturn on February 28th brings a practical and disciplined approach to your work. You are likely to focus on long-term goals, strategic planning, and attention to detail. This is an excellent time to review your professional responsibilities, streamline your workflow, and seek ways to enhance your efficiency and productivity.

The Mars square Jupiter aspect on February 27th brings opportunities for growth and expansion in your career. You may encounter new projects, promotions, or exciting ventures that test your skills and push you out of your comfort zone. Embrace these challenges with enthusiasm and confidence, as they have the potential to propel your professional growth.

However, the Mars square Neptune aspect on February 28th may introduce some uncertainties and potential setbacks. It's crucial to stay grounded, maintain realistic expectations, and exercise caution in making major decisions. Use your intuition and discernment to navigate any complexities that arise, and seek support from trusted colleagues or mentors if needed.

The Venus square Jupiter aspect on February 10th reminds you to find a balance between professional ambition and personal fulfillment. While it's essential to pursue your career goals, don't neglect self-care and maintaining a healthy work-life balance. Nurture your personal relationships and engage in activities that bring you joy and relaxation, as they contribute to your overall well-being and success.

Remember to tap into your innovative and visionary nature throughout the month. Your unique perspectives and ideas have the potential to make a significant impact in your field. Embrace collaboration, think outside the box, and leverage your creativity to find unconventional solutions to challenges.

Finance

The Venus square Neptune aspect on February 25th reminds you to exercise caution and discernment when it comes to financial decisions. Be mindful of potential illusions or unrealistic expectations that could lead to financial risks or losses. It's essential to conduct thorough research and seek expert advice before making any significant investments or financial commitments.

However, the Venus trine Uranus aspect on February 7th brings unexpected financial opportunities and breakthroughs. You may receive a sudden windfall, unexpected bonus, or a lucrative business proposal. Stay open-minded and receptive to these unexpected blessings, as they have the potential to improve your financial standing.

The Mercury conjunction with Saturn on February 28th emphasizes financial discipline and responsibility. This alignment encourages you to review your financial goals, create a realistic budget, and focus on long-term financial stability. It's a favorable time to assess your spending habits, eliminate unnecessary expenses, and establish a solid savings plan.

The Mars sextile Neptune aspect on February 7th invites you to explore innovative and creative ways to enhance your financial situation. Consider alternative sources of income or investment opportunities that align with your unique skills and interests. Your ability to think outside the box can lead to financial breakthroughs and increased prosperity.

It's important to strike a balance between financial prudence and embracing opportunities for growth. The Venus conjunction with Mars on February 22nd reminds you to be proactive and assertive in pursuing your financial goals. Take calculated risks and assert yourself confidently when it comes to negotiating deals or seeking higher-paying opportunities.

Remember to prioritize your financial well-being by practicing self-discipline and avoiding impulsive or unnecessary expenses. Focus on building a strong financial foundation that supports your long-term goals and provides you with a sense of security.

Health

The Sun's semi-sextile with Neptune on February 15th highlights the importance of maintaining a healthy balance between your mind, body, and spirit. This aspect reminds you to prioritize self-care and engage in activities that promote overall well-being.

With the Mercury semi-square Neptune aspect on February 23rd, it's crucial to be mindful of your mental health. Take time for relaxation, meditation, and introspection to combat stress and anxiety. Engaging in activities that stimulate your mind, such as reading, puzzles, or creative pursuits, can help maintain mental clarity and emotional balance.

The Mars square Jupiter aspect on February 27th encourages you to be cautious with physical activities. While you may feel energized and motivated, it's important to avoid overexertion or engaging in high-risk endeavors. Focus on maintaining a consistent exercise routine that suits your fitness level and consult with a healthcare professional before taking on any intense physical challenges.

The Sun conjunction with Mercury on February 28th emphasizes the importance of communication and seeking support for your health needs. If you have any concerns or questions about your well-being, don't hesitate to reach out to healthcare professionals or trusted advisors who can provide guidance and assistance.

Pay attention to your sleep patterns and ensure you are getting sufficient restorative rest. The Venus sextile Neptune aspect on February 13th creates a favorable environment for relaxation and rejuvenation. Consider incorporating calming activities into your daily routine, such as taking warm baths, practicing yoga or meditation, and engaging in hobbies that bring you joy and tranquility.

Nurture your body with nutritious foods and maintain a balanced diet. The Venus square Chiron aspect on February 5th reminds you to be mindful of emotional eating patterns or using food as a coping mechanism. Seek healthier alternatives for managing stress or emotions, such as engaging in physical activities, connecting with loved ones, or practicing mindfulness techniques.

Travel

The Sun's semi-sextile with Uranus on February 26th sparks a desire for exploration and discovery. This aspect encourages you to step out of your comfort zone and embrace opportunities for travel and adventure.

If you have been contemplating a trip, this is an excellent time to plan and make arrangements.

Whether it's a spontaneous weekend getaway or a well-planned vacation, allow your adventurous spirit to guide you. Consider exploring unfamiliar destinations or engaging in activities that broaden your horizons and expand your perspective.

However, it's essential to exercise caution and be flexible with your travel plans. The Mars square Jupiter aspect on February 27th suggests the need for careful planning and risk assessment. Pay attention to travel advisories, weather conditions, and any potential disruptions that may impact your journey. Maintain a backup plan and be prepared for unforeseen changes.

During your travels, embrace opportunities for cultural immersion and connecting with local communities. The Venus quintile True Node on February 20th enhances your ability to form meaningful connections with people you encounter along the way. Engage in conversations, try local cuisine, and immerse yourself in the unique experiences each destination has to offer.

Take advantage of technology to facilitate seamless travel experiences. The Mercury quintile Uranus on February 27th favors using digital tools and applications that make navigation, communication, and trip planning more accessible. Utilize travel apps, language translation tools, and online resources to enhance your travel experience and stay connected with loved ones back home.

Be mindful of your personal safety during your travels. The Mars semi-square Neptune aspect on February 28th highlights the need for vigilance and awareness of your surroundings. Trust your instincts, follow local guidelines, and take necessary precautions to ensure a safe and enjoyable journey.

Remember to balance your desire for exploration with self-care during your travels. Traveling can be physically and mentally demanding, so it's crucial to prioritize rest, hydration, and adequate nutrition. Take breaks, get enough sleep, and listen to your body's needs to avoid travel fatigue or burnout.

Insight from the stars

Embrace change and be open to new experiences, for they hold the key to personal growth. Trust your intuition and follow your heart's desires, even if they diverge from the expectations of others.

Best days of the month: February 5th, 7th, 15th, 19th, 22nd, 24th, and 29th.

March 2024

Horoscope

Dear Aquarius, as March unfolds, you will find yourself immersed in a dynamic and transformative energy that encourages personal growth and evolution. The month begins with the Sun in Pisces, activating your sector of spirituality and introspection. This celestial alignment invites you to connect with your inner wisdom and explore the depths of your psyche. Take time for self-reflection, meditation, and contemplation to gain clarity and insight into your life's purpose.

Mercury, the planet of communication and intellect, also journeys through Pisces, enhancing your intuitive and imaginative faculties. This period is ideal for creative endeavors, spiritual studies, and deepening your understanding of metaphysical subjects. Your intuition will be heightened, and you may receive valuable guidance from your dreams or intuitive flashes.

Venus, the planet of love and beauty, enters Aquarius on March 1st, infusing your relationships with harmony, compassion, and a touch of eccentricity. This is a favorable time to express your authentic self and embrace your unique qualities in your connections with others. Allow your friendships and romantic partnerships to evolve naturally and nurture the bonds that bring joy and fulfillment to your life.

Love

In matters of the heart, March brings a mix of passion, emotional depth, and the need for freedom within your relationships. With Venus in Aquarius, your natural charm and magnetism are amplified, drawing others towards you. You exude a unique and captivating energy that sparks intrigue and fascination. This is an ideal time to embrace your individuality and express your authentic self in romantic connections.

However, Venus square Uranus on March 3rd may introduce some unexpected twists and turns in your love life. Sudden attractions, unconventional relationships, or a desire for greater independence could create an exciting but unpredictable dynamic. Be open to exploring new relationship dynamics, but also ensure clear communication and mutual understanding to maintain harmony.

For those already in partnerships, the influence of Mars in Aquarius heightens passion and ignites a sense of adventure. You and your partner may embark on shared endeavors, explore new hobbies, or engage in intellectual discussions that deepen your bond. However, be mindful of the Mars square Uranus aspect on March 9th, as it may bring some tension or conflicts regarding personal freedom and individual expression. Honest and open communication will be essential in navigating these challenges and finding harmonious resolutions.

If you're single, this is a time to embrace your independence and focus on personal growth. Use your unique qualities and interests to attract like-minded individuals who appreciate your individuality. Don't rush into commitments; allow relationships to unfold naturally and organically.

Career

With the Sun in Pisces, you bring a compassionate and intuitive approach to your work, making you highly attuned to the needs of others. This empathetic nature can be a valuable asset in fields that involve healing, counseling, or creative endeavors.

Mercury's conjunction with Neptune on March 8th enhances your communication skills and imaginative thinking. This is an excellent time for brainstorming, problem-solving, and finding innovative solutions to work-related challenges. Your ability to tap into your intuition and think outside the box will set you apart from your colleagues and make a positive impression on superiors.

However, the influence of Mars in Aquarius may introduce some tension and competitiveness in the workplace. While your assertiveness and drive are commendable, be mindful of conflicts that can arise due to differing opinions and power struggles. Seek diplomatic solutions and use your natural diplomacy and ability to see the bigger picture to defuse any workplace tensions.

The Mercury square Mars aspect on March 14th may bring additional challenges, such as miscommunications or conflicts with colleagues or superiors. It's crucial to remain calm and composed, avoiding unnecessary confrontations. Practice active listening and express yourself assertively yet respectfully to maintain a harmonious work environment.

March 18th marks the Mercury conjunction with the True Node, indicating significant opportunities for professional growth and advancement. This alignment favors networking, collaboration, and forming strategic alliances that can propel your career forward. Pay attention to potential mentors or influential individuals who can guide you on your path to success.

Finance

The alignment of Venus with Saturn on March 21st suggests a need for practicality and discipline when it comes to your financial matters. It's an opportune time to reassess your budget, prioritize your expenses, and consider long-term financial goals.

The Venus square Uranus aspect on March 3rd may introduce some unexpected expenses or financial fluctuations. Be prepared to adapt and make necessary adjustments to maintain financial stability. Avoid impulsive spending and focus on building a solid foundation for your future financial security.

Mercury's conjunction with Neptune on March 8th encourages you to trust your intuition when making financial decisions. Pay attention to subtle cues and messages that guide you towards wise investments or financial opportunities. However, be cautious of potential scams or deceptive financial schemes. Conduct thorough research and seek professional advice before committing to any major financial ventures.

The Sun's semi-square with Pluto on March 21st may bring financial power struggles or conflicts. It's important to maintain financial transparency and avoid getting involved in any unethical practices. Stick to your principles and avoid compromising your integrity for short-term financial gains.

The Venus sextile Jupiter aspect on March 24th brings positive financial prospects and opportunities for expansion. This alignment favors investments, partnerships, or collaborations that have the potential for long-term growth and financial abundance. Consider diversifying your income streams or exploring new avenues for generating wealth.

Health

The Sun's conjunction with Neptune on March 17th highlights the connection between mind, body, and spirit. This alignment emphasizes the need for balance and harmony in your overall well-being. Pay attention to your intuitive signals and listen to the subtle messages your body is sending you. Incorporate practices like meditation, yoga, or mindfulness to foster inner peace and relaxation.

Mars' square with Uranus on March 9th can bring a surge of energy and restlessness. While it may be tempting to push your physical limits or engage in high-intensity activities, be mindful of potential accidents or injuries. Pace yourself and channel your energy into activities that provide a healthy outlet for your dynamism.

The Sun's semi-square with Jupiter on March 19th encourages you to find a balance between indulgence and moderation. While it's important to enjoy life's pleasures, be mindful of overindulging in unhealthy habits or vices. Practice mindful eating, maintain a balanced diet, and engage in regular exercise to keep your body in optimal condition.

Mercury's conjunction with Chiron on March 20th brings attention to emotional healing and self-reflection. Take time to explore any emotional wounds or traumas that may be impacting your overall well-being. Seek support from trusted individuals or consider therapy or counseling to address any underlying issues that may be affecting your health.

Venus' semi-sextile with Chiron on March 26th emphasizes the importance of self-love and self-care. Nurture your relationships and surround yourself with positive and supportive individuals who contribute to your overall well-being. Engage in activities that bring you joy, relaxation, and rejuvenation.

Travel

The Sun's sextile with Jupiter on March 1st brings an optimistic and expansive energy that favors travel for educational or spiritual purposes. Consider destinations that offer opportunities for personal growth, cultural exploration, or spiritual enrichment. Engaging in activities like retreats, workshops, or visiting sacred sites can provide profound experiences during this time.

Mercury's conjunction with Neptune on March 8th heightens your imagination and desire for escapism. It's an ideal period for travel that involves creative or artistic pursuits, such as attending music festivals, exploring art galleries, or immersing yourself in natural landscapes that inspire your creativity.

Venus' conjunction with Saturn on March 21st promotes travel with a focus on structure and responsibility. This may be a suitable time for business trips, networking events, or conferences where you can establish valuable connections and make a lasting impression. Plan your travel itinerary with a keen eye for practicality and efficiency.

Mars' sextile with True Node on March 24th encourages adventurous and spontaneous travel experiences. Embrace opportunities that allow you to step out of your comfort zone, engage in physical activities, or explore new territories. Adventure sports, hiking trips, or exploring unfamiliar cultures can provide a sense of excitement and personal growth.

The Sun's sextile with Pluto on March 21st brings transformative energy to your travel endeavors. Consider destinations with historical significance or places that hold deep spiritual meaning. Exploring ancient ruins, archaeological sites, or engaging in self-discovery retreats can have a profound impact on your personal growth and understanding of the world.

When planning your travel, it's essential to consider the practical aspects such as budget, logistics, and safety. Research destinations thoroughly, check travel advisories, and ensure you have appropriate insurance coverage. Be open to unexpected detours or changes in plans, as they may lead to unexpected and memorable experiences.

Insight from the stars

Embrace the power of your unique perspective. You possess a visionary mind and an innate ability to see beyond the ordinary. Trust your intuition and follow your instincts when making important decisions.

Best days of the month: March 1st, 7th, 12th, 18th, 21st, 24th and 28th.

April 2024

Horoscope

In April 2024, Aquarius, you can expect a dynamic and transformative month filled with opportunities for personal growth and positive changes. The celestial energies align to bring excitement and potential breakthroughs in various aspects of your life. It's a time for self-expression, exploration, and taking calculated risks. Prepare yourself for a month of innovation, social connections, and introspection.

The month kicks off with Mercury forming a semi-sextile aspect with Venus on April 2nd. This alignment brings harmony and ease to your communication skills, enhancing your ability to express yourself clearly and compassionately. It's a great time to have important conversations or negotiate agreements.

As the Sun semi-sextiles Saturn later that day, you may feel a sense of responsibility and discipline guiding your actions. Use this energy to focus on your long-term goals and make steady progress in your personal and professional endeavors. The combination of Aries and Pisces energies brings a blend of assertiveness and intuition to your decision-making process.

On April 3rd, the Sun forms a quintile with Pluto, bringing opportunities for personal transformation and empowerment. You may experience a deepening of self-awareness and a desire to release old patterns that no longer serve you. This aspect encourages you to embrace your personal power and make positive changes in your life.

Mars also forms a quintile with Uranus on the same day, infusing your actions with originality and spontaneity. This aspect stimulates your desire for freedom and independence, prompting you to explore new ways of approaching tasks and challenges. Embrace your unique ideas and embrace your inner rebel.

Venus conjoins Neptune on April 3rd, creating a dreamy and romantic energy in your relationships. This aspect enhances your sensitivity and compassion, making it an ideal time for deepening emotional connections and expressing your feelings. Be cautious, however, not to get lost in illusions or become overly idealistic.

The Sun's conjunction with the True Node on April 4th signifies a significant turning point in your life path. It's a time to align yourself with your true purpose and embrace the opportunities that come your way. Pay attention to synchronicities and intuitive nudges, as they may guide you towards your destiny.

Love

With Venus and Neptune joining forces in Pisces on April 3rd, your love life is infused with a dreamy and compassionate energy. This alignment heightens your intuition and opens the door to deep emotional connections.

If you're in a relationship, this is a time of increased sensitivity and understanding between you and your partner. You may find yourselves engaged in deep conversations, exploring your hopes, dreams, and vulnerabilities. This alignment encourages you to express your love in imaginative and romantic ways, creating a deeper bond between you and your partner.

For single Aquarians, the Venus-Neptune conjunction presents opportunities for new and exciting connections. You may be drawn to individuals who exude an air of mystery or possess artistic and spiritual qualities. However, it's important to maintain a balance between fantasy and reality to avoid idealizing potential partners. Stay open-minded and trust your intuition to guide you towards meaningful connections.

As April progresses, the Sun's conjunction with Mercury on April 11th amplifies communication and intellectual connection in your relationships. This alignment encourages heartfelt conversations, where you and your partner can express your deepest desires and concerns. It's a wonderful time for expressing love through words, whether it be through heartfelt letters, poetry, or engaging discussions.

However, be aware that the Sun's square with Pluto on April 21st may bring power dynamics or intense emotions to the surface. This aspect can trigger deep transformations within relationships, uncovering hidden issues that need to be addressed. Use this opportunity to confront any emotional baggage and foster healthier dynamics in your love life.

Career

The semi-square between Mercury and Mars on April 6th may create some minor challenges in communication and collaboration. It's crucial to remain patient and diplomatic when dealing with colleagues or superiors. Avoid rushing into conflicts and instead focus on finding common ground and compromise.

On April 8th, the Sun's semi-sextile with Jupiter brings a boost of optimism and expansive energy to your professional pursuits. This alignment favors taking calculated risks, exploring new opportunities, and expanding your professional network. Embrace opportunities for growth and showcase your innovative ideas and talents.

The Sun's conjunction with Chiron on April 8th highlights the potential for healing and personal growth within your career. This alignment may bring forward past wounds or insecurities related to your professional life. Use this time to address any self-limiting beliefs and embrace your unique skills and strengths. Self-reflection and self-compassion will lead to increased confidence and success.

As April progresses, the Sun's conjunction with Mercury on April 11th enhances your communication skills and intellectual prowess. This alignment supports negotiations, presentations, and collaborative projects. Your ability to articulate ideas and engage in productive discussions will be instrumental in advancing your career.

The Mars-Saturn conjunction on April 10th reminds you to focus on discipline and perseverance. It's a time for strategic planning, attention to detail, and consistent effort. Hard work and determination will pay off, allowing you to overcome obstacles and achieve your professional goals.

Finance

The conjunction of Venus and Neptune in Pisces on April 3rd may inspire some financial idealism. You might be tempted to make impulsive purchases or invest in speculative ventures. While it's important to indulge your creative and imaginative side, exercise caution and avoid making hasty financial decisions. Take time to assess the long-term consequences before committing your resources.

The Sun's semi-sextile with Jupiter on April 8th brings a positive energy to your financial sector. This alignment signifies potential growth and expansion in your income streams. You may receive unexpected opportunities for increased earnings or find ways to maximize your existing resources. It's an ideal time to explore new avenues for financial stability and seek out professional advice if needed.

The semi-square between Venus and Jupiter on April 10th reminds you to strike a balance between your desires and financial responsibilities. Avoid excessive spending or taking unnecessary risks with your money. It's crucial to maintain a practical approach and make informed choices that align with your long-term financial goals.

The Sun's semi-square with Saturn on April 20th emphasizes the importance of discipline and financial planning. This aspect serves as a reminder to stick to your budget, prioritize saving, and avoid impulsive purchases. Take a realistic view of your financial situation and make strategic decisions that support your long-term financial security.

Health

The semi-square between Mercury and Mars on April 6th may bring a slight increase in mental and physical stress. Take note of any signs of tension or fatigue and make sure to incorporate relaxation techniques into your daily routine. Practice deep breathing exercises, meditation, or engage in activities that help you unwind and release tension.

On April 13th, Mercury's semi-sextile with Uranus encourages you to seek mental stimulation and engage in activities that challenge your intellect. This alignment supports mental agility and problem-solving skills. Consider exploring new hobbies, learning opportunities, or engaging in stimulating conversations to keep your mind sharp and energized.

The Mars-Pluto semi-square on April 13th reminds you to be mindful of power struggles and the impact of stress on your physical well-being. Take breaks when needed, practice stress management techniques, and prioritize restful sleep. Nurturing a balanced lifestyle and healthy boundaries will contribute to your overall health.

The Sun's conjunction with Mercury on April 11th enhances your communication skills, which can positively impact your mental and emotional well-being. Expressing your thoughts and feelings openly, whether through journaling, creative outlets, or engaging with loved ones, can be therapeutic and supportive of your mental health.

It's essential to maintain a balanced approach to your physical health. Pay attention to your dietary habits, ensuring a well-rounded and nutritious diet. Incorporate regular exercise into your routine, choosing activities that you enjoy and that promote both strength and flexibility.

Listen to your body's needs and address any minor health issues promptly. Be proactive about scheduling routine check-ups and seeking medical advice if necessary. Taking a preventative approach to your health will contribute to long-term well-being.

Travel

The Venus-Neptune conjunction on April 3rd infuses your travel plans with a sense of adventure and romance. You may be drawn to destinations that have a mystical or artistic appeal. Consider exploring coastal towns, beach resorts, or cities known for their artistic and cultural heritage. Embrace the beauty of new surroundings and allow yourself to be inspired by the unique experiences you encounter.

The Sun's semi-sextile with Jupiter on April 8th adds a touch of luck and abundance to your travel endeavors. This alignment favors planning trips that offer both personal growth and enjoyment. You may find opportunities to connect with like-minded individuals or participate in group activities that enrich your travel experiences. Embrace spontaneous moments and be open to unexpected encounters that enhance your journey.

If you're planning international travel, be mindful of any travel restrictions or logistical considerations due to external circumstances. Stay updated on travel advisories and follow safety guidelines to ensure a smooth and secure trip. Flexibility and adaptability will be key in navigating any unforeseen changes or challenges that may arise.

If long-distance travel is not feasible during this time, consider exploring local destinations or embarking on day trips to nearby places of interest. Embrace the opportunity to discover hidden gems in your own backyard and appreciate the beauty and diversity of your local surroundings.

Insight from the stars

Aquarius, the stars have a special message for you in April 2024. Embrace your unique quirks and eccentricities, for they are what make you shine. Don't be afraid to think outside the box and challenge the status quo. Embrace your rebellious spirit and let it guide you towards innovative solutions and groundbreaking ideas.

Best days of the month: April 3rd, 8th, 11th, 13th, 19th, 21st, and 28th.

May 2024

Horoscope

As the month begins, Venus squares Pluto on May 1st, signaling a potential shift in your relationships and financial dynamics. This aspect may bring intense emotions and power struggles to the forefront. It's essential to maintain open and honest communication, setting boundaries and respecting the boundaries of others. Be mindful of any hidden agendas or manipulative behavior, and strive for authenticity and balance in your connections.

On May 6th, Saturn's semi-square with Pluto emphasizes the need for discipline and careful planning in your endeavors. This alignment reminds you to assess your long-term goals and make strategic decisions that align with your vision for the future. Avoid getting overwhelmed by external pressures and focus on creating solid foundations for your success.

Mercury's conjunction with Chiron on May 6th brings opportunities for emotional healing and self-reflection. This alignment encourages you to confront and heal any past wounds or limiting beliefs that may be hindering your personal growth. Embrace vulnerability and seek support from trusted friends or professionals if needed. This introspective work will pave the way for greater self-acceptance and empowerment.

As May progresses, the Sun's sextile with Saturn on May 7th enhances your discipline and work ethic. This aspect supports your career endeavors, allowing you to make steady progress towards your professional goals. Embrace structure and prioritize your responsibilities to maximize your productivity and achieve long-term success.

The Sun's conjunction with Uranus on May 13th ushers in an energy of excitement and innovation. This alignment stimulates your desire for freedom and independence, urging you to embrace your unique ideas and approaches. It's a time for thinking outside the box, taking risks, and embracing change. Trust your intuition and allow your creativity to flourish.

Towards the end of the month, the Sun's trine with Pluto on May 22nd empowers you to transform and transcend limitations. This aspect brings deep insights and the ability to tap into your personal power. Use this energy to release old patterns, embrace your strengths, and pursue your passions with renewed vigor.

Love

The square between Venus and Pluto on May 1st may bring intensity and power struggles in your romantic interactions. It's important to approach these situations with open and honest communication, setting healthy boundaries, and addressing any underlying issues. This aspect encourages you to delve into the depths of your relationships, uncovering hidden dynamics, and working towards transformation and healing.

On May 10th, Venus semi-squares Neptune, adding a touch of idealism and romance to your love life. You may find yourself yearning for a deep soul connection or indulging in romantic fantasies. However, it's crucial to maintain a balance between idealism and reality. Keep your expectations grounded and communicate openly with your partner to ensure a healthy and authentic connection.

As May progresses, the Sun's conjunction with Uranus on May 13th sparks a sense of excitement and spontaneity in your love life. This alignment encourages you to embrace your individuality and express your unique desires and interests. It's a time to break free from routine and explore new ways of connecting with your partner. Embrace unconventional ideas and allow your relationship to evolve and grow.

The Sun's trine with Pluto on May 22nd deepens the intensity and transformative energy in your love life. This aspect encourages you to face any emotional barriers and let go of patterns that no longer serve you. By embracing vulnerability and being open to change, you can experience profound growth and a renewed sense of passion in your relationships.

For single Aquarians, May offers opportunities to meet someone with whom you share a deep soul connection. Embrace social events, join new communities, and allow yourself to be open to unexpected encounters. Trust your intuition when it comes to potential partners, and don't be afraid to take a chance on love.

Career

The Sun's sextile with Saturn on May 7th enhances your discipline and work ethic. This alignment encourages you to stay focused and committed to your goals. By prioritizing your responsibilities and embracing structure, you can make steady progress and achieve tangible results. Use this time to establish a solid foundation for your professional success.

On May 13th, the Sun's conjunction with Uranus ignites your entrepreneurial spirit and desire for innovation. This aspect encourages you to think outside the box, embrace change, and pursue your unconventional ideas. Trust your intuition and don't be afraid to take calculated risks in your career endeavors. Your unique approach and willingness to embrace new technologies or strategies can lead to breakthroughs and recognition.

The trine between the Sun and Pluto on May 22nd empowers you to tap into your personal power and transform your professional life. This aspect brings deep insights and the ability to overcome limitations. Embrace your strengths and leverage them to make a positive impact. Use this transformative energy to release old patterns, step into leadership roles, or initiate important projects.

Throughout May, it's essential to foster effective communication and build strong professional relationships. Networking opportunities may arise, and collaborations can lead to fruitful outcomes. Embrace teamwork and collaboration while also showcasing your individual skills and contributions.

For those seeking career advancement or considering a career change, May offers favorable energies. Be open to new opportunities, explore avenues aligned with your passions and interests, and be proactive in seeking out growth and development opportunities. Trust your instincts and let your authentic self shine through in professional interactions.

Finance

The square between Venus and Pluto on May 1st may bring about financial challenges and power dynamics. It's important to be cautious and avoid impulsive spending or risky financial decisions during this time. Focus on maintaining a balanced approach and sticking to your budget. Take a closer look at your financial relationships and ensure that they align with your values and long-term goals.

On May 10th, Venus semi-squares Neptune, highlighting the importance of clarity and practicality in financial matters. Be wary of potential illusions or unrealistic expectations when it comes to financial investments or ventures. Take a measured approach, do thorough research, and seek professional advice if needed. Maintaining a realistic outlook will help you make informed decisions and protect your financial interests.

As May progresses, the Sun's conjunction with Uranus on May 13th brings unexpected financial opportunities and a desire for financial independence. Embrace your innovative ideas and think outside the box when it comes to your financial pursuits. Explore new avenues for income generation and be open to non-traditional methods of financial growth. However, ensure that you assess the risks and rewards before taking any major financial leaps.

The trine between the Sun and Pluto on May 22nd enhances your financial acumen and empowers you to make transformative decisions. This aspect encourages you to review your financial strategies and make necessary adjustments. Consider long-term investments, savings plans, or strategies that align with your goals for financial stability and growth. Seek professional advice if needed to maximize your financial potential.

Throughout May, it's important to maintain a practical approach to your finances. Stick to your budget, prioritize saving, and avoid unnecessary expenses. Regularly review your financial situation, track your spending, and identify areas where you can cut back or optimize your resources.

Embrace a mindset of abundance and gratitude for the financial blessings in your life. Practice responsible financial habits, cultivate a healthy relationship with money, and be open to opportunities for growth and prosperity.

Health

The Sun's semi-square with Neptune on May 3rd reminds you to pay attention to your emotional well-being. It's important to address any feelings of overwhelm or stress. Engage in activities that promote relaxation and inner peace, such as meditation, yoga, or spending time in nature. Taking breaks and creating boundaries will contribute to your overall mental and emotional health.

On May 13th, the Sun's conjunction with Uranus sparks a desire for spontaneity and freedom. Embrace physical activities that align with your individuality and bring you joy. Consider trying new fitness routines or outdoor adventures that provide a sense of excitement and invigoration. Be open to exploring innovative approaches to exercise and wellness.

The Sun's trine with Pluto on May 22nd empowers you to embrace transformative changes in your health habits. This aspect encourages you to release old patterns and adopt healthier lifestyle choices. It's a favorable time to focus on nourishing your body with nutritious foods, staying hydrated, and getting sufficient restful sleep. Consider incorporating stress-reducing activities, such as meditation or journaling, into your daily routine.

Throughout May, be mindful of your energy levels and avoid overexertion. Listen to your body's needs and make self-care a priority. Find a balance between work and relaxation to avoid burnout. If you experience any physical discomfort or health concerns, seek professional advice and address them promptly.

Remember that self-care extends beyond physical health. Nurture your emotional well-being by fostering healthy relationships, setting boundaries, and engaging in activities that bring you joy and fulfillment. Cultivate a positive mindset, practice gratitude, and embrace moments of self-reflection.

Travel

On May 13th, the Sun's conjunction with Uranus ignites a sense of adventure and spontaneity in your travel plans. This alignment encourages you to embrace unique destinations and unconventional experiences. Consider exploring off-the-beaten-path locations or engaging in activities that push your boundaries and ignite your sense of discovery.

The trine between the Sun and Pluto on May 22nd adds depth and transformative energy to your travel experiences. This aspect invites you to explore destinations that have a profound impact on your personal growth and transformation. Whether it's a spiritual retreat, a nature-filled adventure, or immersing yourself in a different culture, embrace the opportunities for inner exploration and expansion.

Throughout May, be mindful of any travel restrictions or logistical considerations due to external circumstances. Stay updated on travel advisories and follow safety guidelines to ensure a smooth and secure journey. If long-distance travel is not feasible, consider exploring local destinations or engaging in day trips to nearby places of interest. There may be hidden gems and meaningful experiences waiting to be discovered in your own backyard.

As you embark on your travels, remember to prioritize self-care and well-being. Take breaks when needed, stay hydrated, and be mindful of maintaining a healthy balance between exploration and relaxation. Engage in activities that bring you joy and allow for rejuvenation, whether it's indulging in local cuisine, practicing mindfulness in nature, or immersing yourself in cultural experiences.

Insight from the stars

Embrace the unexpected and trust in your intuition. The path of wisdom lies in being open to change, even if it challenges your comfort zone. Embrace the unique qualities that make you who you are and let them shine brightly.

Best days of the month: May 13th, 16th, 18th, 22nd, 23rd, 25th, and 30th.

June 2024

Horoscope

With Mars in Aries semi-sextile Uranus in Taurus on June 1st, you're infused with a burst of energy and enthusiasm. This combination empowers you to take bold steps towards manifesting your desires and breaking free from any limitations. Use this energetic momentum to pursue your passions and assert your individuality.

The Sun's quintile with Neptune on June 1st enhances your intuitive abilities and sparks creativity. Embrace your artistic side and engage in activities that allow you to express yourself freely. Trust your instincts and pay attention to the subtle messages from the universe.

Mercury's sextile with Neptune on June 2nd deepens your imagination and heightens your communication skills. This aspect encourages meaningful and compassionate conversations. Seek connection and understanding in your interactions with others.

As the month progresses, the Sun's conjunction with Venus on June 4th brings harmonious and loving energy into your life. This alignment enhances your relationships, fostering deep connections and emotional bonds. It's a time to express your affections and appreciate the beauty that surrounds you.

June 8th brings a square between Venus and Saturn, challenging your relationships and financial matters. It's important to approach these areas with patience, maturity, and a willingness to work through any obstacles. Seek practical solutions and communicate openly to find resolution and stability.

The Sun's square with Saturn on June 9th may bring temporary setbacks or responsibilities. Stay focused and resilient, knowing that hard work and perseverance will lead to long-term success. Maintain a positive mindset and trust in your abilities to overcome any challenges.

On June 19th, Mercury's quintile with Chiron invites you to embrace your inner healer. Use your words and intellect to inspire and uplift others. Your insights and wisdom have the power to bring healing and transformation to those around you.

Love

With the Sun's conjunction with Venus on June 4th, a wave of love and harmony washes over your romantic endeavors. This alignment enhances your magnetism and brings a greater sense of appreciation and affection to your relationships. It's a wonderful time to express your love, shower your partner with affection, and create moments of beauty and romance together.

The square between Venus and Saturn on June 8th may present some challenges in your love life. It could bring forth issues of commitment, responsibility, or long-term goals. It's essential to communicate openly and honestly with your partner, addressing any concerns or fears that may arise. Patience, understanding, and a willingness to work through difficulties will strengthen your bond.

June 11th holds the sextile between Venus and Chiron, offering opportunities for emotional healing and growth in your relationships. This aspect encourages vulnerability and authentic communication, allowing for deeper emotional connections and the resolution of past wounds. Take the time to listen and support your partner, fostering an environment of trust and understanding.

As June progresses, the Sun's square with Neptune on June 20th may bring some confusion or illusions in matters of the heart. It's important to maintain clarity and set healthy boundaries to avoid any misunderstandings. Trust your intuition and seek honest communication to navigate these complexities.

On June 26th, Venus squares the True Node, bringing a need for growth and evolution in your love life. Embrace the opportunities for transformation and expansion, even if it requires stepping out of your comfort zone. This aspect may lead to exciting changes and new connections that align with your personal growth.

Throughout June, it's crucial to cultivate self-love and self-care. Embrace your individuality and honor your own needs and desires. When you nourish yourself, you bring a sense of wholeness and fulfillment to your relationships.

Career

With the Sun's conjunction with Venus on June 4th, your charm, charisma, and creative energy shine brightly in the workplace. This alignment enhances your ability to collaborate effectively with others and fosters harmonious relationships with colleagues. Take this opportunity to showcase your talents and share innovative ideas that can elevate your professional standing.

On June 8th, the square between Venus and Saturn may introduce some challenges in your career path. You may encounter obstacles or face limitations that require patience and perseverance. Use this time to reassess your long-term goals, refine your strategies, and focus on building a solid foundation for success. Embrace a disciplined work ethic and remain dedicated to your professional aspirations.

The Sun's square with Saturn on June 9th further emphasizes the need for discipline and commitment in your career. It may bring temporary setbacks or responsibilities that test your resolve. Stay focused on your objectives and maintain a positive mindset. Your perseverance and determination will pave the way for long-term success.

As June progresses, the Sun's square with Neptune on June 20th encourages you to be cautious of illusions or unclear situations in your professional life. Pay attention to details and seek clarity in your work-related endeavors. Trust your intuition and rely on your analytical skills to navigate through any challenges that arise.

June 28th brings Mercury's square with Chiron, presenting an opportunity for healing and growth in your career. This aspect may bring forth past wounds or insecurities that need to be addressed. Use this time for introspection and self-reflection, allowing yourself to heal and release any self-limiting beliefs that may hinder your progress.

Throughout June, stay proactive in seeking professional development opportunities. Embrace new technologies, expand your skill set, and stay updated on industry trends. Your willingness to adapt and learn will contribute to your growth and open doors to exciting possibilities.

Finance

The square between Venus and Saturn on June 8th may bring some challenges and limitations to your finances. It's essential to exercise caution in your spending habits and take a disciplined approach to budgeting. Look for ways to reduce unnecessary expenses and prioritize long-term financial goals.

On June 11th, the sextile between Venus and Chiron brings opportunities for healing and transformation in your financial mindset. This aspect invites you to address any underlying fears or insecurities surrounding money. Embrace a growth-oriented mindset and seek guidance or education to expand your financial knowledge.

As the month progresses, the Sun's square with Neptune on June 20th may bring some financial uncertainties or illusions. Be vigilant in financial transactions and avoid making impulsive decisions. Trust your intuition and seek professional advice if needed to ensure clarity and financial stability.

June 26th brings Venus square the True Node, signaling the need for growth and evolution in your financial pursuits. This aspect may present opportunities to diversify your income sources or explore new investment avenues. Stay open-minded and be willing to adapt to changing circumstances.

Throughout June, it's crucial to maintain a balanced approach to your finances. Focus on building a solid financial foundation by saving, investing wisely, and planning for the future. Seek opportunities to increase your income through additional streams or innovative ideas.

Health

With the Sun's square with Saturn on June 9th, it's essential to pay attention to any potential physical or mental fatigue. This aspect may bring temporary challenges that require rest and rejuvenation. Listen to your body's signals and ensure you're getting enough sleep, nourishing yourself with nutritious foods, and engaging in regular exercise.

On June 11th, the sextile between Venus and Chiron presents an opportunity for emotional healing and self-care. Take the time to address any emotional wounds or stressors that may be affecting your overall well-being. Engage in activities that bring you joy, practice self-compassion, and seek support from loved ones or professionals if needed.

The Sun's square with Neptune on June 20th may bring some emotional or mental fog. It's important to prioritize clarity and maintain healthy boundaries. Practice mindfulness and engage in activities that promote relaxation and stress reduction, such as meditation or spending time in nature.

Throughout June, focus on finding a balance between work, rest, and play. Avoid overexertion and give yourself permission to take breaks when needed. Incorporate stress management techniques into your daily routine, such as deep breathing exercises or engaging in hobbies that bring you joy.

On June 26th, Venus squares the True Node, emphasizing the need for self-love and self-care. Pay attention to your emotional well-being and practice self-compassion. Engage in activities that nurture your soul, whether it's through creative expression, connecting with loved ones, or indulging in self-care rituals.

Travel

The square between Venus and Saturn on June 8th may present some challenges or delays in your travel plans. It's important to stay flexible and adaptable, as unexpected circumstances may arise. Have contingency plans in place and maintain a positive mindset, embracing any changes as opportunities for growth and new experiences.

On June 11th, the sextile between Venus and Chiron infuses your travels with opportunities for emotional healing and personal growth. As you explore new places and cultures, be open to connecting with the local communities and immersing yourself in their traditions. Engage in activities that expand your understanding of different perspectives and allow for personal transformation.

As the month progresses, the Sun's square with Neptune on June 20th reminds you to remain attentive to the details of your travel arrangements. Ensure that you have all necessary documents, make backup copies of important information, and stay vigilant against potential scams or miscommunications. Trust your intuition and seek clarity if anything seems unclear.

Throughout June, allow yourself to embrace the spontaneity and freedom that travel brings. Engage in activities that align with your adventurous spirit, whether it's exploring nature, trying local cuisine, or engaging in thrilling experiences. Embrace the unknown and step outside of your comfort zone, as these experiences have the potential to broaden your perspectives and create lasting memories.

June 26th brings the square between Venus and the True Node, indicating the potential for serendipitous encounters and connections during your travels. Embrace these opportunities to meet new people and expand your network. Engage in meaningful conversations and be open to learning from others' experiences.

Insight from the stars

Embrace laughter and don't take life too seriously. Allow your inner child to play and find joy in the simple pleasures. Embrace the magic of the universe and trust that it has amazing surprises in store for you.

Best days of the month: June 4th, 9th, 14th, 20th, 24th 26th and 29th.

July 2024

Horoscope

July 2024 brings a mix of opportunities for Aquarius. With Jupiter in Gemini semi-square Chiron, you may experience a heightened sense of introspection and a desire to heal past wounds. This introspection can lead to breakthroughs and personal growth. The Sun's semi-square with Uranus on July 1st may bring unexpected changes or disruptions, urging you to embrace flexibility and adaptability.

Mercury's trine with Neptune on July 2nd enhances your intuitive and creative abilities, making it an excellent time for artistic pursuits and spiritual exploration. However, be mindful of Mercury's opposition with Pluto on July 3rd, as it may bring intense conversations or power struggles. Practice diplomacy and maintain open-mindedness during this time.

The Sun's square with the True Node on July 2nd prompts you to reflect on your relationships and connections with others. This aspect encourages you to align your personal growth with the collective journey, fostering meaningful connections and collaborations.

Love

In matters of the heart, Aquarius, July 2024 brings a mix of emotional depth and romantic possibilities. Venus trine Saturn on July 2nd fosters stability and commitment in relationships. It's a favorable time to strengthen the bonds with your partner through open communication and shared responsibilities.

However, Venus square Chiron on July 6th may bring up some emotional vulnerabilities and past wounds in relationships. Take this opportunity to address any unresolved issues, seek healing, and deepen the connection with your loved one.

Career

July 2024 presents exciting opportunities for career advancement and professional growth, Aquarius. Mercury quintile Uranus on July 7th ignites your innovative thinking and brings fresh ideas to the table. Embrace your unique perspective and explore creative solutions to challenges at work.

Venus sextile Jupiter on July 8th enhances your charm and networking skills. It's an excellent time to expand your professional contacts, collaborate with like-minded individuals, and seek new opportunities for career advancement.

Mercury sextile Jupiter on July 8th further supports your communication skills and intellectual pursuits. Use this time to engage in fruitful discussions, pitch your ideas, and present your work with confidence.

Finance

In the realm of finances, Aquarius, July 2024 encourages you to be cautious and diligent in your money matters. Venus opposition Pluto on July 12th warns against impulsive spending and financial risks. Take a closer look at your financial decisions and ensure they align with your long-term goals.

Mars sextile Neptune on July 20th brings a harmonious blend of action and intuition. It's a favorable time to trust your instincts when making financial choices. Consider seeking advice from trusted professionals and conducting thorough research before making significant investments.

Health

Your well-being is of utmost importance in July 2024, Aquarius. The Sun square Chiron on July 15th highlights the need for emotional healing and self-care.

Take time to nurture your emotional well-being through practices such as meditation, journaling, or seeking the support of a therapist or counselor.

The Mars-Uranus conjunction on July 15th may bring a surge of energy, but also a need for balance and grounding. Pay attention to your physical limits and avoid overexertion. Incorporate activities like yoga, meditation, or outdoor walks to maintain a sense of inner balance.

Travel

July 2024 offers opportunities for travel and exploration, Aquarius. The Jupiter quintile Neptune on July 18th brings a sense of adventure and expands your horizons. Consider planning a trip to a destination that ignites your curiosity and allows you to connect with different cultures and perspectives.

The Sun sextile Uranus on July 18th encourages spontaneity and embracing new experiences. Step out of your comfort zone and engage in activities that challenge and inspire you. Whether it's a weekend getaway or a more extended journey, travel can provide valuable insights and broaden your worldview.

Insight from the stars

Remember to embrace the spontaneous and playful side of life. The Venus quintile Mars on July 22nd encourages you to enjoy the pleasures of the present moment and let your passions guide you.

Best days of the month: July 1st, 8th, 15th, 18th, 20th, 22nd and 31st.

August 2024

Horoscope

In August 2024, Aquarius, you are entering a transformative and introspective period. The planetary aspects indicate a time of self-reflection, personal growth, and inner exploration. It's an opportunity to delve deep into your emotions, dreams, and desires to gain a better understanding of yourself.

Mars sextile True Node on August 1st energizes your connections and collaborations. It's a favorable time to engage in teamwork, networking, and social interactions that align with your goals and aspirations.

Venus quintile Jupiter on August 2nd brings a harmonious blend of love, abundance, and optimism. This alignment enhances your relationships, fostering joy, and harmony in your personal life.

The Sun's biquintile Saturn on August 4th emphasizes the importance of discipline and structure in achieving your long-term goals. Use this time to evaluate your commitments, set boundaries, and make practical plans for the future.

Love

In matters of the heart, Aquarius, August 2024 offers a mix of passion and introspection. Venus square Uranus on August 2nd may bring unexpected changes or disruptions in your relationships. It's crucial to embrace flexibility and open communication to navigate any challenges that arise.

On August 15th, Venus biquintile Chiron encourages healing and emotional growth in your relationships. Use this opportunity to address any past wounds, deepen connections, and foster a greater sense of empathy and understanding with your partner.

Career

August 2024 presents significant opportunities for professional growth and career advancement, Aquarius. Mars sextile Neptune on August 6th enhances your intuition and creativity in the workplace. Trust your instincts and explore innovative approaches to problem-solving and decision-making.

Mercury biquintile True Node on August 12th enhances your communication skills and fosters collaboration. This alignment supports teamwork, effective networking, and the sharing of ideas. Use this time to connect with influential individuals who can help you further your career goals.

Finance

In the realm of finances, Aquarius, August 2024 calls for a balanced approach and prudent decision-making. The Sun quincunx Saturn on August 10th highlights the need for responsible financial planning and management. Evaluate your budget, prioritize your expenses, and consider long-term investments that align with your financial goals.

Venus trine Pluto on August 29th brings favorable financial opportunities and the potential for increased wealth and resources. However, exercise caution and seek professional advice before making any major financial commitments.

Health

Your well-being is of utmost importance in August 2024, Aquarius. The Sun biquintile Neptune on August 15th encourages a holistic approach to health and wellness. Engage in practices that nurture your mind, body, and spirit, such as meditation, yoga, or creative pursuits.

The Mars square Saturn on August 16th highlights the importance of maintaining a balanced approach to physical activity. Avoid overexertion and be mindful of your limits to prevent burnout or injuries. Incorporate rest and relaxation into your routine to support overall well-being.

Travel

August 2024 offers opportunities for travel and exploration, Aquarius. The Sun quintile Jupiter on August 22nd sparks a sense of adventure and expands your horizons. Consider planning a trip to a destination that aligns with your interests and allows you to immerse yourself in new cultures and experiences.

The Venus trine Uranus on August 27th encourages spontaneity and embracing unique travel experiences. Step out of your comfort zone and explore off-the-beaten-path destinations or engage in activities that challenge and inspire you.

Insight from the stars

Aquarius, as you navigate August 2024, embrace the duality of your nature. Embrace your unconventional side and celebrate your unique perspective. Remember to find a balance between introspection and social connections. Nurture your relationships while also giving yourself space for self-reflection. Above all, remain true to yourself and let your authenticity shine brightly.

Best days of the month: August 2nd, 6th, 12th, 115th, 22nd, 27th, and 31st.

September 2024

Horoscope

Aquarius, September 2024 brings a mix of introspection and external influences into your life. It's a time of deep self-reflection and evaluating your place in the world. The planetary aspects indicate a need for balance and harmony between your personal growth and your interactions with others.

Mercury trine Chiron on September 2nd invites healing and self-awareness. Use this time to address emotional wounds and embrace self-compassion. It's an opportunity to cultivate a deeper understanding of your own vulnerabilities and develop healthier ways of communicating and connecting with others.

The Sun's quintile Mars on September 2nd ignites a surge of energy and motivation. Channel this dynamic force into pursuing your passions and taking bold actions towards your goals. Embrace opportunities for growth and challenge yourself to step out of your comfort zone.

Love

In matters of the heart, September 2024 presents a period of introspection and growth for Aquarius. Venus opposition True Node on September 3rd may bring a temporary sense of imbalance or tension in your relationships. This alignment calls for reassessment of your needs, values, and desires to ensure that your partnerships align with your personal growth. It's important to communicate openly and honestly with your loved ones during this time.

Mars square Neptune on September 3rd requires caution in romantic endeavors. This aspect brings the potential for illusions and unrealistic expectations. It's crucial to stay grounded and focus on clear communication, trust, and shared goals to maintain healthy relationships. Be wary of idealizing or romanticizing situations, and instead, focus on building genuine connections based on authenticity and mutual understanding.

Career

In the realm of career and professional pursuits, September 2024 urges Aquarius to strike a balance between personal aspirations and collaboration. The Sun's opposition Saturn on September 8th highlights the importance of responsibility, discipline, and long-term planning in your career. It's a time to evaluate your professional commitments and ensure that they align with your values and ambitions. Take the necessary steps to achieve your career goals while maintaining a sense of integrity and authenticity.

Mercury square Uranus on September 7th may bring unexpected changes or disruptions in the workplace. It's crucial to embrace flexibility, adaptability, and innovative thinking to navigate any challenges that arise. This aspect also encourages you to think outside the box and explore new approaches to your work. Embrace opportunities for learning and growth, and be open to unconventional ideas that can propel your career forward.

Finance

September 2024 calls for Aquarius to exercise prudence and focus on financial stability. Venus sesquiquadrate Uranus on September 8th warns against impulsive spending or risky investments. It's essential to practice financial discipline, create a budget, and seek expert advice before making any major financial decisions. Take a cautious approach and prioritize long-term financial security over short-term gains.

Mercury trine Pluto on September 24th brings opportunities for financial growth and empowerment. This alignment encourages strategic planning, research, and analysis in your financial endeavors. Consider exploring new avenues to increase your income, such as investments or passive income streams. However, make sure to conduct thorough research and seek professional advice before making any significant financial commitments.

Health

Your well-being takes center stage in September 2024, Aquarius. The Sun's trine Uranus on September 19th ignites a sense of vitality and promotes innovative approaches to health and self-care. Embrace new exercise routines, wellness practices, and explore alternative healing modalities that resonate with you. It's a favorable time to break free from old habits and adopt healthier lifestyle choices.

Mars trine Saturn on September 30th emphasizes discipline and consistency in maintaining your physical and mental well-being. Use this energy to establish a structured routine, set realistic health goals, and stick to them. Prioritize self-care and establish healthy boundaries to manage stress effectively.

Travel

September 2024 presents opportunities for travel and exploration, Aquarius. Venus trine Jupiter on September 15th brings positive experiences in travel, adventure, and expanding your horizons. Consider planning a trip or embarking on a new adventure that allows you to explore different cultures, broaden your perspectives, and create lasting memories.

However, with Mercury square Jupiter on September 21st, it's crucial to remain practical and consider logistics when making travel plans. Pay attention to details, double-check reservations, and have contingency plans in place to mitigate any potential challenges. Embrace spontaneity but also exercise caution and preparedness during your travels.

Insight from the stars

Remember, the path to success lies in combining innovation with grounded action. Trust your inner wisdom and take bold, inspired steps towards your dreams.

Best days of the month: September 2nd, 7th, 15th, 19th, 24th, 26th and 30th.

October 2024

Horoscope

October brings a dynamic and transformative energy to Aquarius, setting the stage for personal growth, exciting opportunities, and deep introspection. As the month unfolds, you will find yourself navigating a journey of self-discovery, with the potential for significant breakthroughs and profound transformation in various aspects of your life.

The Sun's sesquiquadrate Uranus on October 4th marks the beginning of a period of self-reflection and the urge to break free from old patterns and limitations. This alignment encourages you to embrace change, challenge the status quo, and explore new possibilities. It is a time of personal reinvention and pushing the boundaries of your own potential. Embrace this energy and use it to fuel your ambitions and embark on innovative projects that align with your true passions and purpose.

In summary, October presents Aquarius with a period of transformative growth, both personally and professionally. Embrace the energy of change, nurture your relationships, seize career opportunities, and prioritize self-care. Trust your intuition, embrace your individuality, and embark on new adventures with a sense of excitement and open-mindedness. By harnessing the transformative energies of the month, you can pave the way for a fulfilling and empowering chapter in your life.

Love

In the realm of love, October presents Aquarius with a series of intense and transformative experiences. The celestial alignment of Venus biquintile True Node on October 3rd brings forth a soulful and karmic energy that is bound to deepen your connections with others. During this time, you may encounter individuals who have a profound impact on your life, and you might even find yourself drawn to soulmates or kindred spirits. It is essential to embrace these encounters with an open heart and mind, as they have the potential to catalyze personal growth and spiritual awakening.

As the month progresses, the harmonious trine between Venus and Mars on October 8th adds a passionate and romantic dimension to your relationships. This alignment ignites the flames of desire and strengthens the bond between you and your partner. You will experience a heightened sense of sensuality and a deep longing for emotional intimacy. Use this time to express your desires openly and explore new levels of connection with your loved one. For those who are single, this alignment can bring an exciting encounter that sparks a fiery romance.

However, it is important to maintain a balanced approach in your relationships. The intense energy of October can also bring about challenges and emotional confrontations. The Mercury opposition Chiron on October 8th may uncover old wounds or insecurities within yourself or your partner. It is crucial to approach these sensitive topics with compassion and understanding. Use this opportunity to heal and grow together, strengthening the foundations of your relationship.

Career

In October, Aquarius can expect a promising and transformative period in their career. The Sun's sesquiquadrate Uranus on October 4th encourages you to break free from conventional work patterns and explore innovative ideas. This aspect pushes you to embrace change and step out of your comfort zone. It is an excellent time to challenge existing systems, propose new strategies, or even consider alternative career paths. Your unique and forward-thinking approach will be valued and appreciated by your colleagues and superiors.

The trine between Mercury and Jupiter on October 8th further enhances your communication skills and brings favorable interactions in the workplace. This alignment amplifies your ability to express your ideas, articulate your thoughts, and engage in meaningful discussions. Your persuasive communication style and intellectual prowess will have a positive impact on your professional relationships and can lead to exciting collaborations or opportunities for advancement.

However, it is essential to strike a balance between your innovative ideas and practicality. While it is important to explore new avenues, be mindful of the potential risks involved. Seek advice from mentors or trusted colleagues before making any major career decisions. By combining your unique perspective with a grounded approach, you can navigate the professional landscape successfully and make significant strides in your career journey.

Finance

October urges Aquarius to approach their finances with careful planning and a discerning eye. The square aspect between Mercury and Mars on October 6th serves as a reminder to be cautious of impulsive spending and hasty financial decisions. It is crucial to assess your financial situation realistically and avoid taking unnecessary risks. Create a budget and stick to it, focusing on essential expenses and prioritizing long-term financial stability.

However, the trine between Venus and Saturn on October 4th provides a stabilizing influence on your financial matters. This alignment promotes discipline and practicality in your approach to money. You will find it easier to exercise self-control, resist temptations, and make responsible financial choices. Consider consulting with a financial advisor or expert to ensure that your long-term financial goals are on track and well-protected.

Additionally, the trine between Venus and Mars on October 8th can bring unexpected financial opportunities through collaborations or joint ventures. This aspect favors teamwork and cooperative efforts, which may lead to increased income or financial gains. Be open to exploring new avenues for generating wealth, such as investments or side ventures, but approach them with caution and conduct thorough research before committing your resources.

Health

The sesquiquadrate aspect between the Sun and Uranus on October 4th serves as a reminder to incorporate variety and spontaneity into your fitness routine. Explore different forms of exercise or physical activities that bring you joy and keep you motivated. Consider engaging in activities that promote mental clarity and emotional well-being, such as yoga, meditation, or nature walks.

With the trine between Venus and Mars on October 8th, the energies favor a harmonious and loving relationship with your body. Use this time to pamper yourself and indulge in self-care rituals that nurture your physical and emotional well-being. Focus on maintaining a balanced diet, getting enough rest, and establishing healthy routines that support your energy levels and overall vitality.

However, it is important to be mindful of the potential for stress or emotional overwhelm during the month. Take proactive steps to manage stress levels through relaxation techniques, mindfulness practices, and seeking support from loved ones or professionals when needed. Remember that self-care encompasses not just the physical aspect but also the emotional and mental realms, so prioritize your mental health and emotional well-being alongside your physical fitness.

Travel

The energy of the month encourages you to break free from routine and explore unfamiliar territories. Whether it's a spontaneous weekend getaway or a more significant journey, embrace the spirit of adventure and embrace the unknown.

The trine between Mercury and Jupiter on October 8th enhances your communication skills and facilitates positive interactions during your travels. This aspect supports engaging conversations, cultural exchange, and the potential to form meaningful connections with people you encounter along the way. Be open to new experiences and embrace the diversity of the world around you.

When planning your travels, be mindful of practical considerations and ensure that you have all necessary documents, accommodations, and safety measures in place. Research your destination thoroughly, including local customs and guidelines, to make the most of your travel experience and ensure a smooth journey.

.

Insight from the stars

Remember, Aquarius, that your unique perspective and unconventional approach to life are your greatest assets. Embrace your individuality and dare to be different. Don't be afraid to challenge societal norms and pursue your passions with unapologetic enthusiasm. Trust in your intuition and let your inner visionary guide you. Remember, it is your uniqueness that will propel you to great heights and inspire others to think outside the box.

Best days of the month: October 3rd, 8th, 12th, 15th, 22nd, 24th, and 31st.

November 2024

Horoscope

Dear Aquarius, November 2024 holds a tapestry of celestial events that will greatly influence your life. Brace yourself for a month filled with dynamic energy and transformative experiences. As an Aquarius, you are naturally inclined towards intellectual pursuits and unique ideas, and this month will offer you ample opportunities to express your innovative spirit.

The planetary alignment in November brings a harmonious blend of optimism, intellectual prowess, and emotional depth. Jupiter, the planet of expansion and growth, forms a sextile with Chiron on November 2nd, infusing you with a heightened sense of wisdom and understanding. This alignment encourages you to explore new knowledge and expand your horizons. Embrace this energy by seeking out educational opportunities or engaging in philosophical discussions that broaden your perspective.

On the same day, Mercury forms a trine with Mars, empowering your communication skills and lending you the energy to express your thoughts with clarity and conviction. This alignment favors intellectual pursuits, networking, and collaborative projects. Take advantage of this period to engage in stimulating conversations and connect with like-minded individuals who share your vision.

A significant planetary aspect occurs on November 3rd when Mars opposes Pluto, generating intense energy within you. This aspect may bring power struggles or confrontations, but it also provides an opportunity for deep transformation and personal growth. It is essential to channel this energy constructively, avoiding conflicts and instead focusing on introspection and self-reflection. Use this period to identify and release any destructive patterns or limiting beliefs that hinder your progress.

Love

The opposition between Venus and Jupiter on November 3rd may create a sense of restlessness in your romantic relationships. You may find yourself questioning your desires and seeking greater personal freedom. It is crucial to communicate your needs honestly and compassionately with your partner, ensuring that your quest for independence does not lead to misunderstandings or conflicts.

For single Aquarians, this alignment presents an opportunity to explore new romantic avenues and embrace spontaneous encounters. Allow yourself to step outside of your comfort zone and engage in activities or events where you can meet like-minded individuals. Keep an open heart and mind, as love may come unexpectedly.

As the month progresses, Venus forms harmonious aspects with Chiron, Saturn, and Neptune, bringing a sense of stability and emotional depth to your relationships. These aspects encourage vulnerability, empathy, and authentic connections. It is a favorable time to deepen the bonds with your partner or express your feelings to someone you care about.

If you are seeking a long-term commitment, the semi-sextile between Venus and Pluto on November 11th brings transformative energy to your love life. This aspect may lead to a significant shift in your romantic partnership or bring new insights into your understanding of love. Embrace this opportunity for growth and embrace the changes that arise.

Overall, November encourages you to balance your need for freedom with your desire for emotional connection. By communicating openly, embracing vulnerability, and being receptive to new experiences, you can foster harmonious and meaningful relationships.

Career

The celestial alignments during this month favor innovation, intellectual growth, and collaboration. Prepare yourself for significant breakthroughs and opportunities that can propel your career to new heights.

The trine between Mercury and Mars on November 2nd empowers your communication skills and boosts your intellectual prowess. This alignment encourages you to express your ideas with confidence and clarity, making it an excellent time for negotiations, presentations, or networking events. Your ability to articulate complex concepts and persuade others to embrace your vision is heightened, opening doors to new possibilities.

As the month progresses, the opposition between Mercury and Jupiter on November 18th brings expansive energy to your professional life. This alignment inspires you to think big, explore new territories, and embrace intellectual challenges. You may find yourself drawn to educational opportunities or seek collaborations with individuals who share your passion for innovation and change.

116

Additionally, the harmonious aspect between Mercury and Chiron on November 19th enhances your problem-solving abilities and encourages you to think outside the box. You may discover unique solutions to complex issues or find innovative ways to improve your work processes. Embrace your natural inclination towards unconventional ideas and approaches, as they hold the potential to revolutionize your career path.

Furthermore, the opposition between Mercury and Jupiter on November 18th enhances your persuasive skills and expands your professional network. This alignment presents opportunities for new partnerships, collaborations, or business ventures. Engage in networking events, reach out to influential individuals, and foster connections that align with your professional aspirations.

It is important to note that the opposition between Venus and Mars on November 14th may introduce temporary conflicts or power struggles within your workplace. Practice diplomacy and seek common ground to resolve any tensions. Maintaining a harmonious work environment is essential for your overall productivity and success.

Finance

The celestial alignments highlight the importance of prudent financial management, strategic decision-making, and a balanced approach to wealth accumulation.

The trine between Venus and Chiron on November 3rd augments your financial intuition and offers insights into improving your monetary situation. This alignment encourages you to reflect on your spending habits, reassess your financial goals, and make adjustments that align with your long-term aspirations. Consider seeking advice from a financial advisor or exploring investment opportunities that have the potential to yield fruitful results.

However, it is crucial to exercise caution during the opposition between Venus and Jupiter on November 3rd, as it may bring a desire for extravagant purchases or impulsive spending. Maintain a balanced perspective and evaluate the long-term consequences of your financial decisions. Focus on cultivating financial stability and security rather than succumbing to short-lived indulgences.

The square aspect between Venus and Neptune on November 9th adds a layer of complexity to your financial matters. This alignment may introduce confusion or deception, making it essential to exercise due diligence and avoid entering into dubious financial arrangements. Be cautious with investments and meticulously scrutinize any offers or opportunities that appear too good to be true.

To navigate the financial landscape successfully, embrace the harmonious aspect between Venus and Saturn on November 22nd. This alignment instills discipline, pragmatism, and a long-term perspective. It encourages you to create a solid foundation for your financial future, focus on saving, and establish sustainable practices that support your overall well-being.

Health

The trine between Mercury and Chiron on November 19th empowers your ability to communicate your health needs effectively. It is an ideal time to seek out medical advice, engage in open discussions with healthcare professionals, and explore alternative healing modalities that resonate with you. Trust your intuition when it comes to your well-being and take the necessary steps to address any health concerns.

The sesquiquadrate between Mercury and Mars on November 6th may bring heightened mental and physical energy, but it also introduces the risk of restlessness and potential burnout. It is crucial to find a balance between productivity and self-care during this time. Prioritize regular exercise, incorporate stress-relief techniques into your routine, and ensure you get ample rest to avoid exhaustion.

The opposition between the Sun and Uranus on November 16th may bring unexpected disruptions or changes to your health and daily routines. Remain adaptable and open to adjusting your plans as necessary. Embrace the opportunity to break free from stagnant habits and explore new wellness practices that resonate with your unique needs.

To support your overall well-being, it is essential to establish a routine that nourishes your mind, body, and spirit. Focus on maintaining a balanced diet, incorporating regular exercise, and dedicating time to activities that bring you joy and relaxation. Prioritize mental health by engaging in mindfulness practices, seeking emotional support when needed, and fostering connections with loved ones.

Remember to listen to your body's signals and honor your limits. If you feel overwhelmed or experience persistent health concerns, seek professional guidance. Self-care and self-compassion are vital components of maintaining optimal health and well-being.

Travel

The celestial alignments during this month encourage you to embrace your wanderlust and embark on journeys that inspire personal growth and broaden your perspective.

The sextile between Jupiter and Chiron on November 2nd infuses your travel experiences with a sense of wisdom and spiritual growth. This alignment opens doors to educational and transformative travel opportunities. Consider embarking on a journey that aligns with your interests, whether it involves visiting sacred sites, attending spiritual retreats, or immersing yourself in different cultures. These experiences have the potential to deeply enrich your life and broaden your understanding of the world.

The trine between Mercury and True Node on November 6th enhances your ability to connect with people from diverse backgrounds and engage in meaningful cultural exchanges. If you are planning a trip during this time, embrace the opportunity to meet locals, forge new friendships, and immerse yourself in the local customs and traditions. The connections you make during your travels may have a profound and lasting impact on your perspective and personal growth.

However, it is important to exercise caution and be flexible with your travel plans due to the potential disruptions caused by the opposition between the Sun and Uranus on November 16th. Stay informed about any changes in transportation or travel restrictions and have contingency plans in place. Embrace the unexpected and be open to spontaneous detours or alternative routes that may lead to unexpected discoveries.

Insight from the stars

Balance your desire for freedom with a sense of responsibility and commitment. Cultivate disciplined financial habits and make decisions that align with your long-term aspirations.

Best days of the month: November 6th, 11th, 19th, 19th, 22nd, 27th and 30th.

December 2024

Horoscope

Dear Aquarius, as the year draws to a close, December 2024 presents a blend of transformative energy and opportunities for personal growth. This month, the celestial alignments encourage you to reflect on your past experiences, embrace your unique individuality, and prepare for the new year ahead.

The biquintile between Venus and Jupiter on December 1st enhances your optimism and inspires a sense of joy and abundance. This alignment invites you to celebrate the blessings in your life and foster harmonious relationships. Embrace the holiday season with an open heart, spreading love and cheer to those around you.

As December unfolds, the trine between Mercury and Chiron on December 2nd empowers your communication skills and encourages healing conversations. This alignment offers an opportunity to express your thoughts and emotions with compassion and vulnerability. Engage in deep and meaningful discussions that can lead to personal growth and emotional healing.

The square aspect between the Sun and Saturn on December 4th brings a sense of discipline and responsibility to your life. This alignment calls for careful planning and strategic decision-making. It is a time to assess your goals, establish practical routines, and lay the groundwork for success in the coming year. Embrace the lessons of perseverance and determination as you navigate any challenges that arise.

In matters of the heart, the semi-square between Venus and Saturn on December 5th may introduce temporary tensions or challenges in your relationships. It is essential to approach these situations with patience and open communication. Focus on nurturing the bonds that matter most to you and finding common ground with your loved ones.

The conjunction between the Sun and Mercury on December 5th intensifies your mental clarity and enhances your ability to express yourself effectively. Use this alignment to organize your thoughts, set clear intentions, and engage in meaningful conversations. Your words have the power to inspire and influence others, so choose them wisely.

Additionally, the opposition between Venus and Mars on December 12th may bring temporary conflicts or power struggles in your romantic relationships. It is crucial to find a balance between your individual needs and the desires of your partner. Practice empathy, compromise, and open dialogue to foster harmonious connections.

As the year comes to an end, the sextile between Venus and Chiron on December 23rd offers an opportunity for emotional healing and self-reflection. Take time to assess your emotional well-being and engage in activities that bring you joy and inner peace. Prioritize self-care and set intentions for a fresh start in the upcoming year.

In summary, December invites you to reflect on your past experiences, nurture your relationships, and prepare for new beginnings. Embrace the lessons of discipline and responsibility, communicate with compassion, and prioritize your emotional well-being. The transformative energy of this month sets the stage for a promising start to the new year.

Love

The trine between Venus and Uranus on December 2nd sparks excitement and a desire for freedom in your love life. This alignment encourages you to break free from stagnant patterns and embrace spontaneity within your relationships. Explore new experiences together, engage in adventurous activities, and allow your love to evolve and grow.

However, it is important to navigate the temporary tensions brought by the semi-square between Venus and Saturn on December 5th. This aspect may introduce challenges or limitations within your relationships. Patience, open communication, and a willingness to compromise are essential to maintain harmony and balance.

The opposition between Venus and Mars on December 12th may intensify passions and ignite conflicts. It is crucial to channel this energy constructively, avoiding power struggles and instead embracing healthy communication and compromise. Seek understanding, be open to your partner's perspective, and find creative solutions to any conflicts that arise.

As the year draws to a close, the sextile between Venus and Chiron on December 23rd invites you to heal emotional wounds and foster deeper connections. This alignment encourages vulnerability and open-heartedness, allowing for emotional growth and nurturing bonds. Take time for heartfelt conversations, express your emotions authentically, and listen with empathy to your partner's needs.

For single Aquarians, this month offers an opportunity for self-reflection and personal growth. Embrace the transformative energy and focus on self-love and self-care. Use this time to clarify your desires, set intentions for the type of love you wish to attract, and engage in activities that bring you joy and fulfillment. By nurturing your relationship with yourself, you create a strong foundation for future romantic connections.

Remember, love is a journey of growth and discovery. Embrace the lessons and transformations that arise, communicate with honesty and compassion, and cultivate connections that support your emotional well-being.

Career

In the realm of career and professional pursuits, December 2024 holds opportunities for Aquarius to reflect, reassess goals, and set the stage for success in the upcoming year. The celestial alignments during this month inspire strategic thinking, innovative ideas, and a focus on personal growth within your chosen field.

The trine between Mercury and Chiron on December 2nd enhances your communication skills and encourages deep introspection. This alignment invites you to reflect on your career goals, assess your progress, and identify areas where you can further develop your skills. Engage in self-reflection and seek feedback from mentors or colleagues to gain valuable insights.

The opposition between Mercury and Jupiter on December 4th fuels your intellectual curiosity and stimulates your desire for expansion and growth. This aspect encourages you to think big, embrace new challenges, and consider opportunities that align with your long-term aspirations. Engage in professional development activities, expand your knowledge base, and embrace a mindset of lifelong learning.

The square aspect between the Sun and Saturn on December 4th brings a sense of discipline and responsibility to your professional life. This alignment calls for meticulous planning and strategic decision-making. Take the time to assess your goals, evaluate your progress, and establish practical routines that support your ambitions. Focus on long-term success and remain committed to your chosen path.

Additionally, the sextile between Venus and Neptune on December 17th enhances your creativity and intuition within your career. This aspect opens doors to innovative ideas, imaginative problem-solving, and the ability to inspire others with your unique approach. Embrace your creative instincts and trust in your intuitive guidance to make sound professional choices.

As the year comes to a close, it is important to take time for reflection and set intentions for the upcoming year. Assess your career achievements, acknowledge your growth, and envision the next steps on your professional journey. Embrace the transformative energy of December to lay the foundation for a successful and fulfilling career path in the future.

Finance

In terms of finances, December 2024 encourages Aquarius to approach their monetary matters with prudence, discipline, and a long-term perspective. The celestial alignments during this month highlight the importance of careful planning, responsible decision-making, and finding a balance between financial stability and personal fulfillment.

The biquintile between Venus and Jupiter on December 1st brings an optimistic and abundant energy to your financial matters. This alignment invites you to celebrate the blessings in your life and cultivate a mindset of gratitude. However, it is important to exercise moderation and avoid impulsive spending. Focus on wise financial choices that align with your long-term goals.

The semi-square between Venus and Saturn on December 5th may introduce temporary tensions or limitations in your financial situation. This aspect reminds you to exercise caution, maintain a realistic perspective, and make decisions that prioritize financial stability. Budgeting, saving, and responsible financial management are key to navigating any challenges that arise.

The square aspect between Venus and Uranus on December 28th brings a desire for financial freedom and unconventional approaches to your finances. While this aspect may spark innovative ideas or opportunities, it is essential to carefully evaluate the risks involved. Seek professional advice, conduct thorough research, and weigh the potential rewards against the potential pitfalls before making any major financial decisions.

To navigate your financial landscape successfully, embrace the semi-square between Venus and Neptune on December 17th. This alignment encourages you to be discerning and cautious when it comes to investments or financial partnerships. Avoid making impulsive decisions and scrutinize any offers that appear too good to be true. Maintain a balanced perspective and trust your intuition to guide you towards sound financial choices.

As the year comes to a close, take time to reflect on your financial goals, reassess your strategies, and set intentions for the upcoming year. Focus on long-term financial stability, responsible budgeting, and cultivating a healthy relationship with money. By practicing discipline, exercising caution, and embracing a balanced approach, you can navigate your financial journey with confidence and lay the groundwork for future success.

Health

In terms of health and well-being, December 2024 invites Aquarius to prioritize self-care, emotional well-being, and finding balance amidst the demands of the holiday season. The celestial alignments during this month encourage you to listen to your body, nurture your mental health, and establish healthy routines that support your overall well-being.

The semi-square between the Sun and Saturn on December 4th brings a sense of discipline and responsibility to your health practices. This alignment calls for balanced self-care, ensuring that you prioritize rest, exercise, and nourishing meals. Find a harmonious rhythm that supports your well-being amidst the demands of the holiday season.

The opposition between the Sun and Jupiter on December 7th may bring a tendency towards indulgence or overextending yourself. It is important to maintain a balanced perspective and avoid excesses that can impact your physical and mental health. Practice mindful eating, set boundaries, and prioritize activities that promote relaxation and stress reduction.

The semi-square between Venus and Neptune on December 17th emphasizes the importance of emotional well-being and self-reflection. Take time to engage in activities that nurture your soul, such as meditation, journaling, or engaging in creative pursuits. Connect with loved ones and seek support if needed, as the holiday season can sometimes evoke mixed emotions.

As the year comes to a close, it is essential to reflect on your health goals and set intentions for the upcoming year. Assess your overall well-being, identify areas that require attention, and establish realistic and sustainable habits. Prioritize self-care, engage in activities that bring you joy and relaxation, and foster connections with loved ones to support your mental and emotional health.

Remember to listen to your body's signals and honor your needs. Pace yourself during the holiday season, set boundaries, and find moments of solitude for reflection and rejuvenation. By prioritizing your well-being, you lay the foundation for a healthy and fulfilling start to the new year.

Travel

In terms of travel, December 2024 offers Aquarius opportunities for both adventurous exploration and rejuvenating escapes. The celestial alignments during this month encourage you to embrace your wanderlust, seek new experiences, and find moments of solace and reflection amidst the holiday season.

The sextile between Venus and Jupiter on December 1st infuses your travel experiences with joy, optimism, and a sense of abundance. This alignment encourages you to embark on journeys that uplift your spirit and expand your horizons. Whether it's a short getaway or a more extended adventure, embrace the opportunity to immerse yourself in new cultures, connect with locals, and create lasting memories.

The square aspect between Venus and Uranus on December 28th may introduce unexpected changes or disruptions to your travel plans. Remain adaptable and flexible, as unforeseen circumstances may require adjustments. Embrace the adventure and view detours as opportunities for new discoveries and spontaneous experiences.

As you plan your travels, consider the semi-square between Venus and Saturn on December 5th. This alignment reminds you to be mindful of your budget and practical considerations. Ensure that your travel plans align with your financial goals and prioritize experiences that offer a balance between enjoyment and responsible spending.

For those seeking rejuvenation, the semi-square between Venus and Neptune on December 17th invites you to embark on a retreat or engage in activities that nourish your soul. Explore tranquil destinations, immerse yourself in nature, or dedicate time to relaxation and self-reflection. Use this opportunity to disconnect from the hustle and bustle of daily life and embrace the healing power of travel.

As the year comes to a close, reflect on the travel experiences that have enriched your life and set intentions for future journeys. Embrace the transformative energy of travel, allow it to broaden your perspective, and create opportunities for personal growth and self-discovery.

Insight from the stars

Find joy in simple moments, and set intentions for the new year. Embrace the transformative power of love, communicate openly and compassionately in your relationships, and foster connections that support your emotional growth. Trust the wisdom of the stars as you step into a new year full of possibilities.

Best days of the month: December 2nd, 10th, 19th, 20th, 23rd, 29th and 31st.

Printed in Great Britain
by Amazon